# MOSES MAIMONIDES' TREATISE ON RESURRECTION

# MOSES MAIMONIDES' TREATISE ON RESURRECTION

translated and annotated by
## FRED ROSNER

JASON ARONSON INC.
*Northvale, New Jersey*
*Jerusalem*

First Jason Aronson Inc. edition—1997

10  9  8  7  6  5  4  3  2  1

Library of Congress Cataloging-in-Publication Data

Maimonides, Moses, 1135–1204.
    [Maḳ 'alah fī teḥiyat ha-metim. English]
    Moses Maimonides' Treatise on resurrection / translated and
annotated by Fred Rosner.
    p.  cm.
    Previously published: New York : KTAV, 1982.
    Includes bibliographical references and index.
    "Bibliography of editions, translations, and studies by Jacob
I. Dienstag" : p.
    ISBN 0-7657-5954-3 (alk. paper)
    1. Resurrection (Jewish theology)    I. Rosner, Fred.    II. Title.
BM645.R47M6713 1997
296.3'3—dc20

    96-42496

Manufactured in the United States of America. Jason Aronson Inc. offers books and cassettes. For information and catalog write to Jason Aronson Inc., 230 Livingston Street, Northvale, New Jersey 07647.

# *Contents*

Preface      vii

Foreword to the Second Edition      ix

Foreword to the First Edition      xiii

Previous Editions and Translations      7

Brief Description of the Treatise      15

Moses Maimonides' Treatise on Resurrection      21

The Resurrection Debate
*by Daniel Jeremy Silver*      71

Bibliography of Editions, Translations and Studies
*by Jacob I. Dienstag*      103

Index      121

# *Preface*

Several years ago, I published an English translation of Moses Maimonides' *Introduction to the Commentary on the Mishnah* (Feldheim Publishers, New York, 1975, 235 pp). The famous introduction contains a lengthy digression into prophethood as well as discussions concerning the value and necessity of homiletical exposition, including a protracted dissertation on knowledge and wisdom and understanding of the existence of living and inanimate things and the purpose of the world and all that is contained therein.

Last year, I published a complete translation into English of Maimonides' *Mishnah Commentary on Tractate Sanhedrin* (Sepher-Hermon, New York, 1981, 214 pp) including the all important chapter called *Perek Chelek*. In his lengthy commentary on this chapter, Maimonides discusses fundamental principles dealing with the basic tenets of the Jewish faith including the existence, unity, eternity and incorporeality of God, prophethood and the prophecy of Moses, reward and punishment, the messianic age, and the resurrection of the dead. The present book, an English translation of Maimonides' *Treatise on Resurrection,* is meant to supplement and complement the aforementioned two works.

I am indebted to my good friend and Torah-studying partner, Rabbi Aaron Twerski, Professor of Law at Hofstra University Law School, Hempstead, New York, for writing the Foreword, to Professor Jacob Dienstag of New York City for helpful suggestions, advice, and his bibliography, to Rabbi Daniel Jeremy Silver of Cleveland for permission to reprint chapter seven from his *Maimonidean Criticism and the Maimonidean Controversy 1180–1240* (E.J. Brill, Leiden, 1965), to Mr. William Wolf of

Denver for correcting the manuscript, and to Mrs. Sophie Falk and Mrs. Miriam Regenworm for secretarial assistance.

To my loving wife Saranne, and to my cherished children, Mitchel, Miriam, Aviva and Shalom, I affirm my love and offer my sincere thanks for their extreme patience during the long hours of painstaking work.

Fred Rosner

New York City
Passover 5741

# Foreword to the Second Edition

The reprinting of Maimonides' *Treatise on Resurrection,* as translated by Dr. Fred Rosner, is a great gift to the world of Torah readership. In the work, Maimonides defends himself against the slanderous charges of other Jewish leaders who had accused him of denying bodily resurrection. Why was Maimonides caught among the vicious attacks of his detractors, particularly with regard to the issue of resurrection? After all, a cursory view of the words of the great sage in his commentary on the *Mishnah, Sanhedrin* 10:1 ("Bodily resurrection is one of the fundamentals of the Law of Moses; one who does not accept [resurrection] has no part in the religion, nor any connection with the Jewish people") and in his *Mishneh Torah, Hilkhot Teshuvah* 3:6 ("The following have no share in the World to Come . . . those who deny bodily resurrection . . .") proves that Maimonides clearly affirmed the phenomenon of resurrection. How, then, could his viewpoint be the source of such great controversy?

Aside from the general historical context of the medieval Maimonidean controversies at large, I believe there is another reason that resurrection became a focal point in the famous medieval polemics. The Jews of the time, and indeed, even the Jews of today, have maintained polar viewpoints concerning the underpinnings of Jewish theology. Maimonides himself alludes to these opposite views in this treatise (sections 32 and 42). Some Jews believe that the principles of Torah and those of the human intellect are diametrically opposed. These people seek to find the miraculous in everything, and they flee from rational explanations. The other group denies anything that cannot be explained or fathomed by the human mind, and therefore, this group denies the historicity or reality of any miraculous event whatsoever. Walking between these two groups we find Maimonides, the rationalist, the theologian. The issue of resurrection represents the entire notion of miracles, as resurrection is *the* miracle par excellence. Therefore, any understanding of the specific issue of resurrection must be contained within the context of miracles in general.

Maimonides explains that rationality, the cornerstone of human involvement in Torah, demands that we seek as clear an understanding as humanly possible for physical and metaphysical phenomena. Simultaneously, we must recognize that the Will of God is ultimately beyond complete human comprehension, and it is that Will that effectuates miracles as they are needed. The non-Torah rationalist, in his rejection of God's providence, thereby eschews the notion of the ultimate miracle, bodily resurrection. Since he cannot explain it, it must be false. The ignorant theologian, who clings emotionally to the appeal of miracles, seeks an emphasis and aggrandizement of the ultimate miracle in the writings of Maimonides and does not find it. As a result, Maimonides, caught in the middle, is attacked from both sides. It is significant to note that in this context, Maimonides' *Treatise on Resurrection* is ultimately a synopsis of the great sage's religious philosophy. God's Will controls the existence of the world, and man is able to get but a glimpse of the effects of that Divine Will. Thus, God has established knowable laws of nature yet is capable of interfering with these laws. Man is left to contemplate the laws of nature and God's involvement with them.

There is, I believe, one more related reason that the issue of resurrection was a focal point of heated debate. Again, Maimonides alludes to it himself in this treatise (section 26) by stating that the multitudes of people (and again, this holds true today as well) do not conceive of any existence apart from the physical. This is the reason so many people are afraid of death. It is also the reason that for many, the notion of bodily resurrection is far more important and appealing than is the idea of the World to Come. If the ultimate reward, in the eyes of the people, is bodily resurrection, then why should Maimonides spend so much ink writing about the World to Come and so little on resurrection? It is due to the fact that for Maimonides, bodily resurrection is not viewed within the context of reward. Ultimate reward is to be found in the felicity of the World to Come, an experience of incomparable spiritual enjoyment. The resurrection, on the other hand, is a manifestation of God's great might. It reflects God's ability to interfere with the natural order on the highest level. The reason God would cause resurrection is to be found in the unknowable Divine Will. This view did not and does not sit well with the multitudes who view as real only that which is physical and therefore look to resurrection as the greatest reward for righteousness and not, essentially, as a sign of God's power. Maimonides, however, speaks of resurrection merely as a prophesied event reflecting God's might. It is the World to Come, a philosophically understandable state of the human soul, that is the great recompense.

This ideology of Maimonides on bodily resurrection is reflected in the daily prayer service. The sages refer to the second blessing of the Eighteen Benedictions as *gevurot,* or God's might. The blessing's theme is bodily resurrection, signifying that the ultimate reflection of God's dominance over the creation is His causing of bodily resurrection. The context of the blessing is God's power, not reward for the righteous.

In this short yet important work, Maimonides, by implication, cautions his readers to relate to God in the most human of ways; we must seek to know God through the divine element within us, our intellect, and yet we must always be aware of the limitations of that element. Simultaneously, we must recognize that physical existence is a mere shadow of the metaphysical, the latter being truly real. As Torah knowledge today continues to spread in wonderful ways, it is important to view our commitment to Torah and its ideology from a perspective of wisdom, one that Maimonides, the great leader and sage, reflects in this treatise. May it be the Will of the Creator that upon realizing the idea of God's *gevurah* through the wisdom and guidance of the sages, we may merit witnessing that *gevurah* along with the era when the earth will be full with the knowledge of God.

Rabbi Saul Zucker

# Foreword to the First Edition

I have been given the honor by my close friend and *chavrusa* (Torah-learning partner) to write a foreword to one of his works. For the past two decades Dr. Fred Rosner has dedicated his free time to the translation of the works of Moses Maimonides, known as the *Rambam*. It is a painstaking and exacting task requiring not only erudition and scholarship but also a God-fearing attitude. Translation requires faithfulness to both the spirit and the letter of the work. When one undertakes the translation of the works of the *Rambam,* the mind and spirit are taxed, for every nuance is imbued with meaning.

The translation of the Rambam's *Treatise on Resurrection* at this time is a matter of considerable importance. Dr. Rosner has sought to bring timely questions to the forefront in many of his writings on medicine and *Halacha* (Jewish law). We live today in the era of *Eekvisa Demashicha* (The Pre-Messianic Era). From all sides we hear the steps of the Messiah or *Moshiach*. It is time to turn our attention to Messianic events. It is an expression of our deep faith that we "await his coming every day."

The story is told of the *Malbim* (Rabbi Meir Leib ben Yechiel Micha'el, 1809–1879) that he made reference to specific years in which he believed that there was special reason to believe that the time was propitious for the coming of the *Moshiach*. He was asked whether he was not in violation of the Talmud's injunction against *"Mechashve Ke'etzin"* (those who reckon the exact year in which the *Moshiach* will appear). The *Malbim* answered with a parable. He told of a father who took his young son along with him on a rather long trip which was to last several days. Some fifteen minutes into the trip the young child turned to his father and asked: "Father, when are we going to arrive?" The father responded angrily and slapped the child. Several days later the child heard his father ask the coachman: "when are we going to arrive?" The bewildered child asked his father: "why is it that when I asked the question you slapped me and now you ask the selfsame question?" To this the father responded: "Don't you see my son, when you asked the question we had just started on a very long trip. If the question of when we were going to arrive would be asked every few minutes we would all lose our patience. I, however, asked the question now when we are about to arrive. It is correct and proper to ask the question at this time."

The appearance in English of a work on the Resurrection of the Dead — a phenomenon of Messianic times — in this era is, thus, even more welcome. It permits us to focus on the happenings of the immediate future. May God grant that we be worthy to welcome the Redeemer and experience the events which attend his coming.

My message would normally conclude at this point. However, the opportunity of this writing permits me to set forth the possible reconciliation of the views of the *Rambam* and others whose opinions about the Resurrection seem divergent. The position of the *Rambam* is that the Resurrection will take place with the soul re-entering the body and that the newly constituted body will function normally. He differentiates this state from that which will take place in *Olam Habbo* (the world to come) in which souls without physical bodies will exist in an angelic state.

It would appear at first blush that the thrust of the kabbalist Moshe Chayim Luzzatto (1707–1746), known as *Ramchal,* in the work *Derech Hashem* is otherwise. He argues that the function of physical death is to cleanse the body from Original Sin (*Chet Odom Horishon*). The return of the soul to the "Soul World" (*Olom Haneshomos*) after death serves the function of permitting the soul to return to its pure and enhanced spiritual state. The power of the soul was diminished in order for it to enter the body and function in a physical body. And thus the interlude between death and the Resurrection allows for the embellishment of its true

spiritual powers. The Resurrection is the event in which the puri-
fied body and the enhanced soul come together. This is the essence
of *Olom Habbo* (the world to come).

Perhaps the two views are irreconcilable. But, there is evidence that the soul-body theory and the pure-soul theory are
closer than we might expect. Rabbi Yaakov Emden (1697–1776),
in seeking to reconcile the views of Nachmanides (1194–1270) and
the *Rambam,* notes that at the final stages of Messianic times the
purification of the body will be such that it will become angelic in
nature. Indeed, *Ramchal* (Luzzatto, *vide supra*) indicates in *Sefer
Hakllalim* that in Messianic times there will be a progression of
physical purification such that the body will be subserviant to the
soul and progress to further levels of purification.

These matters involve *Rozay Hatorah* (the mysteries of
Torah). However, they challenge us to performance in this world
where spiritual excellence is demanded of us. One's ability to perceive and attain spiritual heights in the world to come is directly
proportional to one's attainment here and now.

May God grant that the merit of bringing the words of the
*Rambam* to those who have been foreclosed by language barriers
from studying them, bring to my good friend and colleague Dr.
Fred Rosner and his family, the blessings of Almighty God,
blessed be He, in spiritual and in material things. And may we all
together walk hand in hand to greet *Moshiach Tzeedkainu,* (the
Messiah, our Righteous one), Amen.

Rabbi Aaron David Twerski
9 Adar II, 5741

# Previous Editions
# and Translations

According to Moritz Steinschneider,[1] the original Arabic version of Maimonides' *Treatise on Resurrection (Maqala Fi Teḥiyyat Ha-Metim)*, written in 1191, is lost. Only Samuel Ibn Tibbon's Hebrew translation *Ma'amar Teḥiyat Hametim* is known and was first edited in 1629 (actually 1569, see below). Steinschneider further states that Manuscript Neubauer #2496 in the Bodleian Library has two forewords to this translation. In the first, Ḥarizi states that an anonymous scholar translated this "Epistle" (Hebrew: *megillah*) into Hebrew but not clearly. This Hebrew version was then translated back into Arabic. The latter Arabic version was retranslated into Hebrew for Meir ben Sheshet ha-Nasi. There then follows the foreword of the Arabic translator Joseph ben Joel, a friend of Samuel ibn Tibbon. Steinschneider points out, however, that there is no known mention of this double translation.

In his definitive 1939 edition of Maimonides' *Treatise on Resurrection*,[2] Joshua Finkel states that until recently the Arabic original of this treatise has been known only from two quotations. The first, a fifteen word sentence, was cited by Munk in 1842 from Tanḥum Yerushalmi's *Murshid*; the second, a lengthy excerpt found in Abraham ben Solomon's commentary on the former prophets, was published by Steinschneider in 1880 in his *Hebraeische Bibliographie*. In 1931 and 1933, the Library of the Jewish Theological Seminary of America acquired two Yemenite manuscripts of Maimonides' *Treatise,* and in 1935 it also appeared in the Catalogue of the Hebrew Manuscripts in the British Museum. None of the three, continues Finkel, is complete in itself, but together they form an entirety.

7

On the other hand, Samuel Ibn Tibbon's Hebrew translation of the *Treatise* is available in a considerable number of manuscripts; so numerous, according to Finkel, that the seven manuscripts which he used for his edition are only a modest fraction of those extant. Finkel edited the original Arabic and Samuel Ibn Tibbon's Hebrew translation and glossary based on six Arabic and seven Hebrew manuscripts. Finkel's critical apparatus, notes and introduction are indispensable and make this the definitive Arabic and Hebrew edition of the *Treatise*.

The first printed Hebrew edition of Maimonides' *Treatise on Resurrection* appeared in Venice in 1546, the second in 1569 in Constantinople, and the third in Basel in 1629. Since then, other editions have been published including the editions of Fuerth (1651), Amsterdam (1712 and 1714), Hanau (1715), Leipzig (1848 and 1859), Warsaw (1855 and 1877), Koenigsberg (1858), London (1886), Jerusalem (1961), and Tel-Aviv (1970), among others. The *Treatise* was translated into English by Morais in 1859.[3] This translation is quite poor, rather free and loose and without commentary or annotation. Excerpts in English also appeared in 1957.[4]

In his critical edition, Finkel[2] raises many literary problems in connection with the manuscripts and comments about the alleged double translation, first from Arabic into Hebrew by Samuel Ibn Tibbon, then back into Arabic by Joseph ben Joel and finally the retranslation of the Joseph ben Joel version into Hebrew by Judah al-Ḥarizi. Finkel points out that the Neubauer Hebrew manuscript (allegedly representing the Ḥarizi translation) begins with a short panegyric on Maimonides similar to that in the *Tahkemoni*. The manuscript continues as follows: This epistle, the secret of the resurrection of the dead was sent by Maimonides in Arabic to (the Jews of) every nation and (Jewish) community. He who translated it into Hebrew obscured the matter and "did not clear the road of stones"; and it was translated back from our language (Hebrew) into a clear and elegant Arabic. It was "emptied from vessel into vessel and wandered in exile until it was redeemed" by being retranslated into Hebrew . . . in honor of the *Nasi* R. Meir ben Sheshet.

Finkel's edition reproduces in appendices these two introductions as well as three distichs which follow in which the earlier Ibn Tibbon translation is spoken of disparagingly and that of Ḥarizi is highly lauded. After his own introduction, Ḥarizi cites the introduction of Joseph ben Joel to the latter's Arabic translation of Ibn Tibbon's Hebrew version. The gist of Joseph's statement, in Finkel's words, is as follows:

"I received your letter asking me to translate the late Maimonides' Essay in which he refuted the arguments of the arrogant Talmudists who had dared plagiarize his *Treatise on Resurrection,* but, unfortunately, I am not in possession of the Essay. Our accomplished versatile, esteemed and loyal friend, Samuel Ibn Tibbon, upon receiving a copy of it from Maimonides, contrary to the express wish of the author, did not transmit it to me in the original but in the translation he had made of it. Since however, this translation, because of the limitations of the Hebrew tongue was far from lucid, a friend of mine, one of the literati, asked me to retranslate it into Arabic. I did so with the knowledge that my work is imperfect. . . ."

Based upon the above account, Finkel[2] raises a multitude of questions: Did Maimonides really send his treatise to (the Jews of) all nations and to every Jewish community? Did Ḥarizi really write the beginning of the account? If he did, would he quote his *Tahkemoni* poem, or conversely, as indeed the case may be, would he transplant the poem into his *diwan* . . . Is a secondary Arabic and a tertiary Hebrew translation of our *Treatise* probable? What accounts for the abrupt change of writers in the Introduction? If Maimonides sent his treatise to (the Jews of) every nation and to every Jewish community, how is it that Joseph ben Joel could not find a copy of it? Would Maimonides ask Ibn Tibbon to pass on to Joseph the *Treatise* he had sent him? Would Ibn Tibbon dare to act contrary to Maimonides' wish? If he did, how would Joseph get wind of it and how would he still call Ibn Tibbon "loyal

friend?" ... The *Nasi* R. Meir ben Sheshet and the translator
Joseph ben Joel are otherwise unknown personalities. Are we,
therefore, justified in assuming that they are fictitious characters?

Finkel asserts that although his intent is not to subject these
questions to a minute examination, "the questions in their aggre-
gate eloquently testify to the confusion and inconsistencies of the
report." Finkel concludes that Ḥarizi had no hand in the translation depicted in the Neubauer manuscript. Finkel does admit,
however, that it is possible, although unlikely, that a genuine
Ḥarizi translation, now lost to us, was prepared by him and that
the copyist, not finding it in the defective manuscript he had
copied, concocted one of his own or substituted one that he
thought was Ḥarizi's or might pass as such.

In 1940, the year after Finkel's definitive edition of Maimonides' *Treatise* was published, Baneth, in an article entitled "R.
Judah al-Ḥarizi and the Chain of Translations of Maimonides'
*Treatise on Resurrection,"*[5] took strong issue with Finkel's conclu-
sions. Baneth quotes an earlier writer, Y. Zona (*Tarbiz* Vol. 10; pp
135–154 and 309–332) who said that Ḥarizi never translated either
Maimonides' *Guide for the Perplexed* or his *Treatise on Resurrection* because Ḥarizi's version differs not at all from the Ibn Tibbon
translation. Baneth disputes Zona's assertions and claims that
Ḥarizi in fact translated both of Maimonides' aforementioned
works. Baneth attempts to answer all the questions raised by Finkel. Baneth concludes that Ḥarizi did in fact retranslate into
Hebrew the secondary Arabic translation of Joseph ben Joel. In
another article a year later,[6] Baneth offers textual corrections to
Finkel's Arabic edition and provides clarifications of some of the
difficult passages in Ibn Tibbon's Hebrew translation by referring
to the original Arabic text.

In 1960, Mordecai Dov Rabbinowitz published a new fully
annotated Hebrew edition of Maimonides' *Treatise*[7] with a lengthy
(123 pages) introduction about the various translations of the treatise and the controversy surrounding it. Rabbinowitz restates the
two introductions from the Neubauer manuscript which suggest
that four separate versions of Maimonides' *Treatise on Resurrec-*

*tion* seem to have existed: the original Maimonidean Arabic, the Ibn Tibbon Hebrew translation of the original, the Joseph ben Joel Arabic translation of the Ibn Tibbon version, and the Ḥarizi translation of the Joseph ben Joel version. Rabbinowitz cites Finkel who disputes the four version theory and who considers the sequence of events unlikely and improbable and who suggests that an anonymous later copyist fabricated the whole confusing story. Rabbinowitz also cites Zona (*vide supra*) who concludes that Ḥarizi prepared his Hebrew version directly from the Ibn Tibbon Hebrew translation by modifying and rewriting parts of the Ibn Tibbon version in more easily understandable Hebrew.

Rabbinowitz also cites Baneth who accepts as historical fact, albeit unusual and improbable, the retranslations into Arabic by Joseph ben Joel and back into Hebrew by Ḥarizi as described above. He states that jealousy or anger on the part of Ibn Tibbon at Ḥarizi for the latter's temerity in translating Maimonides' *Guide for the Perplexed* after Ibn Tibbon had already translated it led Ibn Tibbon to keep for himself the Arabic original of the *Treatise on Resurrection* which he had received from Maimonides and not to share it with others. It is possible that the Arabic manuscript which Ibn Tibbon received was the only one which reached Western Europe since there is no extant Arabic manuscript of this work from Europe; all known Arabic manuscripts are from Yemen except for a small fragment found in the Cairo *genizah*. It is thus possible, continues Baneth, that even Joseph ben Joel did not receive an original Arabic version. Since Ibn Tibbon's Hebrew was difficult to comprehend by the masses of people, Joseph was asked to retranslate Ibn Tibbon's Hebrew version into a simple and understandable Arabic. For those whose native tongue was Hebrew, Ḥarizi was then asked to prepare an easily comprehensible Hebrew translation of the Joseph ben Joel Arabic version since Ḥarizi had no access to the original Arabic version of Maimonides.

Rabbinowitz also cites Y.L. Teicher who wrote a sensational article entitled "Literary Forgery in the Thirteenth Century" (*Melilah Kovetz Meḥakrim,* Manchester, 1944). Teicher claims that

Maimonides' *Treatise on Resurrection* is a forgery and that the translations of Ibn Tibbon and Harizi never happened. Rather, the *Treatise* represents a literary forgery which was composed no earlier than 1254, fifty years after the death of Maimonides, and also after the deaths of both Ibn Tibbon and Harizi. Teicher asserts that the *Treatise* was originally written in Hebrew and that this version was circulated among Jewish communities as the Ibn Tibbon translation of an original Arabic version written by Maimonides. This Hebrew version was translated into Arabic by Joseph ben Joel, perhaps in Yemen. According to Teicher, it is the latter Arabic version which was edited by Finkel. Later, the Joseph ben Joel Arabic version was retranslated by an unknown translator who called himself Harizi.

Rabbinowitz takes no sides in the dispute as to the correctness or lack thereof of the arguments set forth by Finkel, Zona, Baneth or others. The Rabbinowitz edition[7] is based on the Leipzig published version. Rabbinowitz says he also consulted the definitive Finkel edition as well as the notes of Baneth.[6]

In 1972, Joseph Kafih published yet another edition[8] of Maimonides' *Treatise on Resurrection*. Kafih's edition contains the original Arabic with a new Hebrew translation and commentary based on a newly discovered manuscript from Yemen. Kafih states that his grandfather possessed two manuscripts of Maimonides' *Treatise on Resurrection*. These manuscripts were estimated to be approximately 200 years old. To Kafih's chagrin, both were lost among the books that were stolen from him during his emigration from Yemen to Israel in 1949. However, God "provided the cure before the affliction." Just prior to Kafih's leaving Yemen, a manuscript came to his attention which was sold by its owner to a book dealer who was about to take it out of Yemen. This manuscript was estimated to be 500 years old and was comprised of numerous writings including the *Treatise on Resurrection*. Since there was no time to engage a copyist, Kafih and a colleague sat in his grandfather's synagogue in Yemen, one next to the other on either side of the manuscript and each copied one column at a time, page after page, until they had copied the entire work which they then returned to its owner. This manuscript is reproduced in the original Arabic in Kafih's edition. He claims that it is nearly identical to the manuscript which Finkel identifies as his Arabic manuscript *zayin*. Kafih further states that Finkel's Arabic manuscripts *ḥeth* and *teth* are full of errors.

Kafih's edition also contains a new Hebrew translation which he himself prepared in "simple Hebrew." He states that he was careful to be faithful to the original because he opposed very free translations since a more literal translation more accurately reflects the intentions of the author. The Kafih Hebrew version is fully annotated. In an introductory footnote, Kafih points out the interesting observation that all known Arabic manuscripts of Maimonides' *Treatise on Resurrection* came from Yemen and not a single manuscript emanated from Europe or from the West or from any other Eastern country.

Kafih asserts that there is no basis at all to believe that Maimonides' *Treatise on Resurrection* is a forgery. Both Samuel Ibn Tibbon and Judah Ḥarizi who lived during the era of Maimonides translated it into Hebrew and both translations are extant. The style and language throughout the treatise are those of Maimonides. We have a tradition from our ancestors, continues Kafih, that the *Treatise* arrived in Yemen in Maimonides' own handwriting and it is from this original version that scribes made copies which were then widely disseminated throughout Yemen.

There is also no basis, continues Kafih, for the legendary assertion which originated with the words of Ḥarizi that after Samuel Ibn Tibbon's Hebrew translation, the original Arabic was lost and was not available until a man named Joseph ben Joel retranslated it into Arabic and Ḥarizi translated from that translation. According to Kafih, these assertions are certainly in error and have no basis in fact. Ḥarizi had the true original Arabic version before him. He also clearly had before him the translation of Samuel Ibn Tibbon. In order to avoid the latter's wrath as happened when he translated the *Guide for the Perplexed*, Ḥarizi fabricated the legend to justify his use of words and phrases from the Tibbon translation.

The present translation is based primarily upon the editions of Finkel,[2] Rabbinowitz[7] and Kafih.[8] There are two major types of translations. One is where an attempt is made to render as closely as possible the flavor and sense of the original work. The other type of translation is where one tries in a loose manner to present the content of the original work, but where one uses the syntax and style of the language into which one is translating. The present translation attempts to follow the former approach.

After completion of this translation, Professor Jacob Dienstag called my attention to the 1973 unpublished master's thesis of Milton S. Polinsky, submitted to the faculty of the Bernard Revel Graduate School of Yeshiva University. Polinsky translated Finkel's Arabic edition of Maimonides' *Treatise on Resurrection* and provided an introduction and notes. Polinsky explains the meaning of the term *maqala* (treatise) and contrasts it with the word *ḥibur* (composition) which is used to describe Maimonides' *Mishneh Torah*.

## References

1. Steinschneider, M. *Die Arabische Literatur Der Juden.* Frankfurt A.M., J. Kauffmann. 1902. p. 210.

2. Finkel, J. *Maimonides' Treatise on Resurrection (Maqala Fi Teḥiyyat Ha-Metim)* New York. American Academy for Jewish Research. 1939. 44 pp (Eng) and 42 pp (Hebr)

3. Morais, S. A Discourse on the Resurrection of the Dead by Maimonides. *Jewish Messenger* No. 11 (Sept. 16, 1859), pp 82–83; No. 12 (Sept. 23, 1859), pp 90–91; No. 13 (Sept. 27, 1859) p. 98; No. 14 (Oct. 7, 1859), p. 106; and No. 15 (Oct. 12, 1859), p. 114.

4. Minkin, J.S. *The World of Moses Maimonides with Selections from His Writings.* New York–London. Yoseloff. 1957. pp 402–405.

5. Baneth, D.Z., *R. Jehuda Al-Ḥarizi Ve-Shalshelet Ha-Targumim Shel Ma'amar Teḥiyat Ha-Metim Le-Rambam.* Tarbiz (Jerusalem) Vol. 11, No. 3–4, April-July 1940. pp. 260–270.

6. Baneth, D.Z. *LeNusach Ma'amar Teḥiyat Ha-Metim Shel Ha-Rambam Ule-Targumo. Tarbiz* (Jerusalem). Vol. 13, No. 1, Oct. 1941. pp 37–42.

7. Rabbinowitz, M.D. *Iggrot Ha-Rambam* — Jerusalem. Mossad Harav Kook, 1960. pp 197–393.

8. Kafih, J. *Iggrot Rabbenu Moshe ben Maimon.* Jerusalem. Mossad Harav Kook, 1972. pp 61–101.

# Brief Description
## of the Treatise

Maimonides' *Treatise on Resurrection,* written in 1191, is an extended controversialist discussion of the problems of God's unity, the Messianic Age, resurrection, and the world to come.[1] Maimonides had already briefly mentioned resurrection of the dead in his *Commentary on the Mishnah* (Tractate Sanhedrin, Chapter *Ḥelek*) which he wrote in 1168. Here he lists resurrection as one of the thirteen fundamental principles or articles of the Jewish faith. Brief statements on resurrection also appear in his famous *Mishneh Torah,* composed in 1178. For example, in *Hilchot Teshuvah,* Maimonides states that those who deny the resurrection of the dead have no share in the world to come.

Because of the brevity of his comments on resurrection in his *Commentary on the Mishnah* and *Mishneh Torah,* Maimonides was asked to expand and amplify his view on this subject. Controversy regarding his views on this subject arose because he espoused a view contrary to the prevailing one which held that resurrection of the dead and the world to come are a single continuum of spiritual existence.[2] Maimonides' view, on the other hand, is that the resurrection of the dead includes not only spiritual but also physical resurrection and that the world to come which is separate from and will follow the resurrection will be wholly a spiritual world with spiritual beings without corporeality.

Maimonides describes the events which led to the composition of his *Treatise on Resurrection* in the latter part of the introduction. They are summarized by Finkel[3] as follows:

After the *Mishneh Torah,* his *magnum opus,* had become known in many lands, it was brought to his attention that one of the pupils of the Academy in Damascus happened to declare openly his disbelief

in the resurrection of the body, basing his denial on some statements in our author's code. His colleagues present on the occasion
attempted to disprove his assertion by citing Biblical verses and
Rabbinic statements to the contrary, but he in turn defended his
position by objecting to a literal interpretation of them. Maimonides ignored the incident on the assumption that such a flagrant
misunderstanding of his teaching was singular and unlikely to
recur. However, in the year 1189, he received a letter from Yemen in
which the writer, *inter alia,* also complained of the fact that the
denial of resurrection was rife among many of his correligionists,
that in support of their heretical view they ascribed an allegorical
purport to the Biblical and Rabbinic statements regarding resurrection, and that they further fortified their denial by some passages in
the works of Maimonides himself. In view of this, the writer
requested a Responsum for the clarification of these mooted points.
Maimonides complied with the request. He intimated that the gist
of his reply was that resurrection of the dead is a basic creed, that
Scriptural references to it are not wise to be allegorized, and that life
in the world to come is to supersede the intermediate state of existence after resurrection. Maimonides thought that this explanation
would suffice, but in the year 1191 he received letters from Babylonia informing him that an inquirer of Yemen had sought advice
on the same problem from Samuel ben Ali, the head of the Bagdad
Academy, whereupon the latter composed for the Yemenites an
impromptu essay on the subject in which some of Maimonides'
eschatological views were sharply assailed. After a while the essay
itself reached Maimonides. The latter, in a few general remarks,
deprecates his opponent's uncritical use of the many edifying Rabbinic utterances concerning the life beyond, and proves his incom-
petence and utter confusion in matters philosophical. Here his
rejoinder to Samuel virtually ends; it is a refutation of general
method rather than specific arguments. Indeed, barring one more
severe censure of the Bagdadian for having falsely accused him of
denying the explicit mention of resurrection in the Bible, he does
not again refer to him directly in the remainder of the Treatise.

Maimonides was faced with the problem that resurrection is
not in accordance with nature and therefore cannot be proved by

philosophy. It is substantiated by revelation. Maimonides makes a rigid demarcation between the Messianic Age in which events retain their physical context, and the world to come where existence is spiritual only.[1]

Maimonides explains why he spoke at length in his *Mishneh Torah* about the world to come but only wrote briefly about resurrection of the dead. Repeating things often does not make them more true nor is the truth diminished if it is only stated once.[4] There are no physical bodies in the world to come, only spiritual beings similar to angels. Angels have intellect. Those who believe that angels are corporeal are in error but are not called heretics. We know of the existence of angels and the eternity of the soul both as basic beliefs and by intellectual or philosophic deduction.[4]

Denial in miracles is heresy, continues Maimonides. Intellectuals try to explain miracles as supernatural events whereas Rabbinic sages attempt to explain them as natural phenomena. Maimonides explains that the Biblical phrases which pertain to resurrection are allegorical and are not to be understood literally because even then nature will not change. The immortality of the soul is a natural phenomenon whereas the resurrection of the dead is a miracle. He explains the Scriptural phrases which seem to contradict the resurrection and states why the Torah does not mention nor allude to this subject.[4]

In his *Treatise on Resurrection,* Maimonides repeats that he firmly believed in resurrection, and that he regarded it as one of the cardinal principles of Judaism. In all his works, he maintained, he had never uttered a single word to the contrary. Whoever, therefore, represented him as having denied this doctrine — he argued — was either deliberately or unconsciously misquoting and misinterpreting him.[5]

As to the reason why he had dealt with the subject so sketchily, he explained that this was a matter of religious belief and therefore not susceptible to philosophical proof. It was not his custom, he said, to bolster up facts with arguments. He had always aimed at brevity. To convince people of what they already knew to be the truth would have been a foolish waste of words: "If I were able to summarize the entire Talmud into a single chapter, I would not write two chapters on it." In short, the proof of the resurrection of the dead is as unnecessary as the proof of the existence of the living. Both are facts. He who believes in creation must also believe in resurrection. The restoration of life to the individual is certainly no greater miracle than the giving of life to a whole universe. He who made the world out of nothing can bring us back out of nothing into the world. Resurrection is a miracle, to be sure. But miracles are natural laws which our reason has not as yet learned to understand.[5]

The problem of the immortality of the soul, however, is quite another matter and is capable of philosophical proof. Immortality means the life of the unbodied soul in its pure spiritual state. After the death of the body, the soul assumes an existence not unlike that of the angels. "You may accept this theory, if you wish," continues Maimonides, "or else you may reject it. Whatever may be your conclusion, I will respect you for it if you have come to it as a result of serious deliberation."[5] According to one recent writer,[6] the accusations that Maimonides did not believe in the resurrection of the dead are evidence of his failure to bring about a different religious orientation. One should read Maimonides' *Treatise on Resurrection* as a tragic and angry confession of failure. This treatise reflects the religious implications involved in the confrontation of reason with tradition. To understand the conflict between reason and revelation as pertaining solely to the legitimacy of different sources of knowledge, is to miss completely the spiritual implications of this conflict. Maimonides clearly shows the difference between a belief in resurrection which depends upon acceptance of Divine miracles and a belief in the world to come which does not. This understanding of the world to come is in harmony with what he writes in his *Mishneh Torah* (*Hilkhot Shemitah Ve-Yovel* 13:13). See also *Hilkhot Issurei Bi'ah* 14:3–5 where the polemical context is evident.[6]

In his *Guide for the Perplexed* 3:31 and 37, and in his *Treatise on Resurrection*, Maimonides offers a historical understanding of the Biblical descriptions of reward and punishment. In *Helek*,

Maimonides provides both a psychological and philosophical explanation of Biblical and Rabbinic promises of reward and punishment. In his exoteric work, *The Treatise on Resurrection,* Maimonides applies the same method to explain why the doctrine of the resurrection of the dead was only mentioned in the book of Daniel. This shows that he believed that the masses would not be upset to know that later Jewish history represents a higher stage of spiritual development than Biblical history.[6]

In the body of his *Treatise,* Maimonides states that some people are disturbed by his remark in the *Mishneh Torah* that, among other things, the Messiah should not be expected to resurrect the dead. They thought that this was a flat contradiction to his statement in the Commentary on *Ḥelek* that resurrection is a principle of faith. But if the Messiah is not to bring the dead back to life, it does not follow that neither will God. Indeed He may achieve this at any time, whether before, after or during the lifetime of the Messiah.

At the conclusion of his *Treatise,* Maimonides once again emphasizes the fact that his *Treatise* contains nothing that he had not already propounded elsewhere. Nevertheless, he added discussions of two subjects not heretofore covered in his other writings. He attempts to show that various Biblical phrases do not, as some suppose, disprove resurrection. The interpretation of *if a man die, may he live again?* (Job 14:14) is compared to *shall we bring you forth water out of this rock?* (Numbers 20:10), that is to say, both are considered to be miracles, not natural events. The second discussion relates to the question as to why resurrection is not mentioned in the Pentateuch.

Finkel[3] summarizes Maimonides' theory that the bodies of the righteous will be resurrected at the beginning of the Messianic era, but upon its termination, will die again to enjoy everlasting existence in spirit only. Similar theories were propounded by Abraham bar Ḥiyya and Ibn Ezra. An exhaustive critical analysis of Maimonides' *Treatise on Resurrection* was published by Finkel.[7] Lengthy discussions of the controversy surrounding Maimonides' *Treatise* are available in the writings of Finkel[3,7], Silver,[1] Rabbinowitz,[2] and Kafih.[4] Silver's chapter on the Resurrection Debate is reprinted in this book.

## References

1. Silver, D.J. *Maimonidean Criticism and the Maimonidean Controversy, 1180–1240.* Leiden. E.J. Brill, 1965. pp 37 to 38 and 109 to 135.

2. Rabbinowitz, M.D. *Iggrot HaRambam.* Jerusalem. Mossad Harav Kook. 1960. pp 197 to 393.

3. Finkel, J. *Maimonides' Treatise on Resurrection (Maqala Fi Teḥiyyat Ha-Metim.* New York. American Academy for Jewish Research. 1939. pp 49 (Eng) and 42 (Hebr.).

4. Kafih, J. *Iggrot-Rabbenu Moshe ben Maimon.* Jerusalem. Mossad Harav Kook. 1972. pp 61 to 101.

5. Münz, J. *Maimonides. The Story of His Life and Genius.* Boston. Winchell-Thomas. 1935. pp 111 to 113.

6. Hartman, D. *Maimonides. Torah and Philosophic Quest.* Philadelphia. Jewish Publ. Soc. Amer. 1976. pp 227 to 230.

7. Finkel, J. Maimonides' Treatise on Resurrection: A Comparative Study. in *Essays on Maimonides. An Octocentennial Volume.* Edit. S.W. Baron. New York. Columbia Univ. Press. 1941. pp 93 to 121.

# Moses Maimonides'
# Treatise on Resurrection

Translated and annotated
by
FRED ROSNER

*In the Name of the Lord, the Everlasting God*[1]

All the words of my mouth are in righteousness,
There is nothing perverse or crooked in them.[2]
They are all plain to him that understandeth,
And right to them that find knowledge.[3]
A prudent man concealeth knowledge,
But the heart of fools proclaimeth foolishness.[4]

## I

1. Said Samuel ben Yehuda[5] ibn Tibbon: the great Sage, Rabbi Moses ben Maimon, may his memory be blessed, said: it is not at all rare that a person intends to elucidate a fundamental principle[6] in plain and simple language and attempts to eliminate all doubts and to remove the need for interpretation, — yet ignorant people[7] understand exactly the opposite of the words which the writer sought to explain. Such a situation occurred in relation to the words of Almighty God, namely: when the master of the prophets[8] intended to inform us that Almighty God is One and there is no second unto Him, and to erase from our minds[9] the false view, which is the belief of the dualists,[10] he clearly stated the following

fundamental principle: *Hear O Israel, the Lord is our God, the Lord is One.*[11] The Christians[12] cite this Biblical phrase as proof to their contention that God is three in that they assert: it is stated the *Lord,* and it is stated *our God,* and it is stated *the Lord,* there are thus three names; then it is stated *One,* proving that they are three and that the three are one. Heaven forbid![13]

**2.**   And if such misinterpretations occur in relation to the words of the Lord, may He be blessed, certainly all the more so can such a thing occur in regard to the words of a human being[14] as happened to some people[15] in the interpretation of our words expressing one of the fundamental principles of the Torah. We intended to comment on an important principle to which the people did not pay attention,[16] as a result of which the people doubted another clearly explained fundamental principle of our faith[17] about which there is no doubt.[18] When we prepared ourselves[19] to write compositions[20] expounding the Torah and explaining its precepts, we did so to fulfill the will of the Lord, may He be blessed and not to receive reward from human beings, nor for the honor;[21] rather we did so to straighten[22] and to explain and to make understandable[23] the words of the Sages of the Torah, of blessed memory, who preceded us, to those of limited understanding. This was our intent. And it appears to us that we elucidated[24] and simplified remote and profound subjects and we gathered and connected widely scattered and separated topics. And we know that we feel relieved in any event; that is to say, if, the matter is as we had thought and we (correctly) simplified and elucidated and gathered in a manner never before done by anyone who preceded us, then we have succeeded in being useful to people and the reward comes from the Lord, may He be blessed.[25] But if the matter is not so, and if our words did not add any clarification nor simplification over that which our predecessors wrote, we will at least receive recompense from the Lord[26] and we have (the knowledge that) our intentions were noble[27] and the Holy One, blessed be He, judges men by their intention.[28]

**3.**   It is this objective[29] which brought my tongue and my hand to compose (this essay) in the manner we set forth[30] as mentioned above in regard to gathering and explaining (these profound matters). And when we prepared ourselves[31] to this (task) we saw that it was not appropriate to carry out our original intent; namely, to explain and to elucidate the details of our faith[32] and to omit the fundamental principles without explaining them and without justifying their truthfulness. On the contrary,[33] we met a man who was regarded[34] as one of the wise men of Israel and, who, may God be my witness,[35] was well versed in the law and in the intricacies of the Torah according to his conceptions (inculcated unto him) from an early age, — yet he was still in doubt as to whether God is corporeal with eyes, hands, feet and intestines as He is depicted in Scriptures, or whether He is not corporeal.

**4.** Indeed, other people that I met from some lands unequivocally proclaimed Him to be corporeal and denounced as a heretic[36] anyone who believes[37] the opposite, and they call him a sectarian[38] and an epicurean,[39] and they cite many passages[40] (in their support which they understand) literally. And I have heard similar things about some people that I have not met.[41] And when I realized, in regard to these (people) who had totally gone astray,[42] that they were elderly[43] and thought that they were wise men of Israel but were, in fact, the most ignorant of all human beings and more perverse in their ways than animals, and their minds were already filled with the senseless prattle of doting old women and with worthless ideas like (those of) young children[44] and women, — we saw that we must elucidate, in our theological writings, fundamental Torah principles in (simple) narrative form[45] and not in the form of citing proofs.[46] For the citation of proofs in regard to those fundamental principles[47] requires expertise in many sciences of which the Talmudists[48] know none at all as we have explained in *The Guide for the Perplexed*.[49] We have chosen (this approach) so that the truths (of our Torah) will at least be accepted by the masses.[50]

## II

**5.** And in the *Introduction to the Commentary on the Mishnah*[51] we mentioned certain fundamental principles which one should accept[52] concerning prophecy and fundamental essentials of (our) tradition and that in which every teacher[53] of the oral law must believe. In the chapter *Chelek,*[54] we also explained fundamental tenets regarding the beginning (of the world) and the ultimate recompense, that is to say regarding the unity of God[55] and the world to come[56] and other cornerstones of our faith.[57]

And we did the same in our *magnum opus* which is known as the *Mishneh Torah*[58] so that its excellence is only appreciated by those religious and wise people of our faith who admit the truth, and who have a positive disposition[59] and recognition of the ways[60] of this composition, and who have an understanding of the diversity of these matters which I gathered there and how I arranged them. In it[58] we also cited all the fundamental principles of the written and oral law.[61] Our intent in all this was that those who are called scholars of the law[62] or wise men[63] or geniuses[64] or whatever they are called, should build their ideations[65] on basic Talmudic principles, and that their Torah should be in good order[66] and their Talmudic learning systematically arranged.[67] All this should be rooted in Torah principles.[68] They[69] should not abandon the knowledge that there is a God[70] because of their rejection;[71] rather, they should apply their great efforts and their zealousness to achieve (moral and spiritual) perfection, and to come closer to their Creator. They should not strive for the type of perfection sought by the masses.[72]

**6.** Among the fundamental principles to which we call attention is the world to come. And we began to speak of the existence of the world to come[73] and were quite lengthy (in our remarks). And we cited proofs from the words of the Bible and proofs from the words of the Rabbis of blessed memory. And we explained that which should be explained to intelligent people. And in the chapter *Chelek*[74] we commented and made known the reason why we placed such emphasis to elucidate the (subject of the) world to come without (elucidating) the resurrection of the dead. And we said that we have only observed people engaged in discussions of the resurrection of the dead: "will they arise naked or in their clothes?"[75] and similar questions.

**7.** However, the world to come is totally forgotten.[76] Further-more, we explained there[77] that the resurrection of the dead is one of the cornerstones of the Torah of Moses our Teacher of blessed memory, but it is not the ultimate goal. Rather, the ultimate goal is the world to come and all this (lengthy discussion concerning the world to come) is to clarify the great doubt which is pondered (by the masses), i.e., that there is no reward or punishment (described) in the Torah except in relation to the present world, and that there is no reward or punishment clearly mentioned in relation to the world to come. And we elucidated from the words of the Torah, according to the Rabbis' interpretations thereof, that the Torah's intent in regard to reward is to the ultimate goal which is the life in the world to come,[78] and in regard to punishment is to the ultimate end which is extinction[79] from the world to come.[80] And these very subjects are those which we elucidated and also explained at great length in our *Composition* in *Hilchoth Teshuvah.*[81]

**8.** But in the chapter *Chelek* we explained — as anyone who delves therein will observe — that after we spoke at length about the world to come, we asserted that the resurrection of the dead is a cornerstone of the Torah and that there is no portion[82] for him that denies that it is part of the Torah of Moses our Teacher,[83] but it is nevertheless not the ultimate goal. So, too, in our *Composition*[84] we enumerated those who do not have a share in the world to come, and we listed them (again) by number and said that they are twenty-four[85] for fear lest a copyist omit one of them and someone say that we did not mention him. Among the twenty-four that we enumerated there is one who denies the resurrection of the dead. And when we mentioned the world to come, we also explained there[86] that it is the ultimate goal and we said as follows: "and this recompense is such that there is none higher and a bliss beyond which there is none more blissful."

**9.** We have also explained[87] that in the world to come there is no corporeal existence, as the Sages, of blessed memory, said: "there is no eating and no drinking and no sexual intercourse (in the world to come)".[88] It would be false, however, to assume that a person has these organs for no purpose; Heaven forbid, God would not create anything for naught.[89] For if a person would have a mouth and a stomach and a liver and sex organs but not eat and not drink and not procreate, then his existence would be absolutely for naught. A person should not argue with these essentials[90] concerning which there are logical proofs through simple expositions which are worthy of being said before women in the house of a mourner.[91]

**10.** There are some who contradict our opinion[92] by saying: behold, Moses and Elijah lived for a time without eating or drinking[93] although they had physical bodies; so will be people in the world to come. *Let it not come unto you, all ye that pass by; behold and see:*[94] the organs of Moses and Elijah, of blessed memory, were not for naught. Both were men from among the people of this world and ate and drank before and after the miracle (which) was wrought for them. Therefore, how can one compare their (temporary) situation to the enduring state which has no end? Rather, it is as our Sages, may their memory be blessed, said: "to a world which is wholly good, to a world which is wholly long;"[95] how could the body there have organs for naught? And it is known that the body as a whole is, indeed, a vessel for the soul with which to perform all its activities.[96] Not one of these activities exists for people in the world to come. These people[97] are unaware of the enormity of the shame which devolves upon anyone who attributes to God an activity for naught and the creation[98] of organs which have a purpose but for no purpose.

**11.** Indeed, all this came about because of the (false) notion in the minds of the multitude of people who do not believe that there is firm existence except for the physical body.[99] They do, however, believe in that which is not corporeal but is within the body, that is to say, temperaments,[100] but (they believe that) their existence is not as firm as the firmness of the body. Nevertheless, these fools say that that which is not part of the body nor a temperament of the body does not exist at all. Although they may be old they are undoubtedly *weaned from the milk and drawn from the breasts.*[101] For this reason, most of them believe that God is corporeal, for if He were not corporeal, He would not exist to them.[102]

Concerning those who are called wise, — those who are truly and figuratively so, — it is clear to them that anything which is separated from a substance has firmer existence than the substance itself and one should not say "more firm."[103] However, separated existence is the true existence because it is not subject to any manner of change.[104] These are (the wise) to whom it is absolutely clear that God is not corporeal nor a power within a body and, therefore, the level of His existence is the firmest of all.[105]

12.   Similarly, everything that is created separate,[106] that is to say the angels and human intellect, is extremely firm in its existence, and exists longer than any body. For this reason, we believe that angels are not corporeal, and that the people in the world to come have separate souls, that is to say intellects.[107] We have already provided proofs thereto from the Torah in our treatise entitled *Guide for the Perplexed.*[108] But if someone from the multitude of people refuses to believe this and prefers to believe that angels have bodies,[109] and that they also eat because it says in Scripture: *and they ate,*[110] and that people in the world to come also have bodies, we will not be insulted by him for this (belief) and will not consider him to be an infidel and will not stay at a distance from him. May there not be many who profess this folly; if only every fool would limit his folly to this level,[111] we would be confident that his belief does not encompass belief in the corporeality of the Creator.[112] There is no harm if he believes in (the corporeality of) separate creations.[113]

13.   And if one of these fools does not even stop to consider that there is a doubt in this matter and that one should not immediately accept one opinion over the other, but vigorously defends the worldly view[114] and claims that our view is erroneous[115] and alienates us because we believe that angels and people in the world to come do not have corporeality[116] and are devoid thereof, — he is not considered to be a sinner. We have already forgiven him for this and we have explained "our error"[117] to him.[118] They have no lack of literal interpretations of many homiletical expositions to which they point to refute our position. Such is not surprising since it is similar to the many Scriptural passages from the words of the

prophets which, if literally interpreted, would ascribe substance, eyes and ears (even) to God. However, when the impossibilities of these intellectual proofs and demonstrations[119] are established,[120] we will know that the (true) situation is as the Sages, of blessed memory, stated: "the Torah speaks according to the language of man,"[121] except that those demonstrations cannot be understood or grasped by one who believes (only) in corporeality.[122]

**14.** And, furthermore, intellectual proofs which confirm that angels and people in the world to come are devoid of corporeality and that the (Scriptural and/or Rabbinic) references which speak of corporeality are simply metaphors — even these proofs cannot be understood by those who believe that the above[123] have corporeality. How can one portray for them an understanding that the above[123] are devoid of corporeality? Concerning even their very existence, that is to say angels and souls, — the latter referring to people in the world to come, — these (believers in corporeality) think that such existence is only known by derivation from the Torah,[124] and that there is no method of meditation which would prove the existence of angels and (the fact) that souls remain (in the world to come). This situation is similar to one who thinks that he has achieved an understanding of the truth, in one moment,[125] although he has very meager knowledge and made only feeble attempts (at penetrating analysis) and neglected all wisdoms and contented himself with the simple interpretation of the Scriptures[126] as if the Sages of blessed memory had never written in many places in the Talmud[127] that the words of Torah have both revealed and hidden meanings, and that the hidden meanings are referred to as the "secrets of the Torah,"[128] and as if the Sages had never said anything about the secrets of the Torah. Rather, these (believers in corporeality of life after death) may their memory be blessed,[129] reject all these (hidden meanings of Torah) as if they didn't exist.[130] We have already explained in the *Guide for the Perplexed*[131] that which is appropriate[132] for wise men concerning these matters; and we cited all the words of the Sages in this matter[133] and we commented on each citation to reveal (the hidden meaning of) that matter from which we brought evidence to support the truth.

## III

**15.** When this *Composition* of ours[134] became known in various countries and disseminated throughout the land, we were told that a certain scholar[135] in Damascus said that there is no resurrection of the dead and that the soul does not return to the body after it has left it. All his colleagues[136] said to him: how can you say that? And he began citing evidence from what we mentioned in our *Composition*[137] that the ultimate goal is the world to come and that there are no (physical) bodies there. And they[138] began to refute him with evidence that is widely known among the people and (by citing) the words of the Sages in this matter. And he replied that these (words) were all allegorical. And they[138] continued their discussions with him at length.

And when this incident became known to us, we paid no attention thereto, saying that this individual's (opinion) is of no consequence[139] because no one can be so foolish as to find it so difficult to understand what we wrote (clearly in our composition).
**16.** But in the year 1500 of the (Seleucid) era used in documents[140] a letter reached us from the lands of Yemen[141] in which they asked various questions and in which they stated that there were certain individuals in Yemen who had concluded that the body will perish and be lost and that the soul will not return to the body after it has separated from it, and that reward and punishment will accrue only to the soul. They cite as evidence that which we stated concerning people in the world to come.[142] And when they were reminded of the clear and lucid words of the Sages[143] in regard to the resurrection of the dead and some of the words of the prophets,[144] they retorted that these (words) were merely allegorical and explainable in that sense. And the questioner told us that this opinion[145] was widely disseminated among them and that the opposite view[146] was being rejected, and he, therefore, asked us for a reply.

We answered their request and explained to them that the resurrection of the dead is a cardinal principle of the Torah, to wit, the return of the soul to the body which should not be explained (allegorically but accepted literally); and that life in the world to come — after the resurrection of the dead — is as we stated it in the chapter *Chelek,* and we thought that this would be sufficient.

**17.** And during the present year, year 1502 of the era used in documents,[147] letters reached us from some of our colleagues[148] in Babylon. They mention that one of the residents of Yemen had addressed an inquiry concerning these same matters[149] to the head of the Rabbinical College, Rabbi Samuel Halevi who was ordained[150] in Bagdad during our time.[151] He wrote a treatise for them on the resurrection of the dead wherein he represented our words in this matter partly erroneously and falsely and partly in a manner that can perhaps be justified. He attempted to defend our views and restricted his pen somewhat.[152]

After the aforementioned letters, the treatise itself, which was composed by this learned Rabbi[153] in his language, was forwarded to us, and we there saw all the expositions and legends which he had gathered.[154] It is known to everyone that the objective of wise people is not to relate such legends and wondrous deeds in plain language as some women relate (stories) in a mourner's house;[155] rather their objective is to explain (these legends) and to clarify their contexts until they are properly understood by the enlightened or at least partially so.

**18.** More surprising than the amazing views which Rabbi Samuel expresses is the fact that he attributes these views concerning the soul to philosophers, thus proving that he believes that everything which his advisors[156] and their like say about false opinions represents the opinions of philosophers. The most amazing thing of all which we noticed therein, that is to say in that treatise — even though it is entirely amazing — is the fact that Rabbi Samuel declares that scholarly philosophers do not say that it is impossible for the soul to return to the body after it has separated from it but that it is theoretically possible. This is exactly what he says. This treatise proves that those who advised him are scholarly philosophers and that he has no knowledge at all of the ways by which philosophers distinguish between the certain, the impossible and the possible.[157]

He also cites passages taken from the *Treatise on Future*

*Reward* by Ibn Sina[158] and from *al-Mutabir*[159] which were available to him in Bagdad and considers them to be philosophical treatises in their entirety.[160] We have also noted that this learned Rabbi decreed and affirmed that philosophers do not believe in the immortality[161] of souls, and that they argue on this point. I wonder: who are those whom he calls philosophers?

**19.**   And we observed another amazing thing, and that is, that the intellect[162] is not at all mentioned by that learned Rabbi. I do not know whether the soul and the intellect are one and the same thing in this philosophy, or whether the soul remains and the intellect perishes, or whether the intellect remains and the soul perishes. This is the soul about which he says that the philosophers do not know it[163] and that one of their views is that it is the blood.[164] Perhaps, he conceives that the intellect is a property of the body[165] as stated by the advisors[166] whom he considers to be scholarly philosophers. If that be the case, it will certainly perish.[167]

**20.**   Had this learned Rabbi[168] contented himself with just assembling those homiletical expositions and legends and the explanations of those Scriptural verses which become clear by virtue of those explanations, to wit that the resurrection of the dead is explicitly mentioned in the Torah, it would have been fitting and proper, (especially) for a man of his learning. In the final analysis, all that which Rabbi Samuel states (in his treatise), or most of it, has already been said elsewhere, more or less. Our intent in this, our treatise, is not to argue with any of the points included in his treatise, nor even to mention it. Indeed, we have only mentioned it as much as we did out of necessity because of our involvement in the matter as will become apparent to the intelligent reader. Rather, our aim is to provide benefit to the reflecting student, and not to aggrandize or enhance the reputation of any man nor to humiliate or demean anyone. The paths of controversies and destructions (of reputations) are only[169] for those who wish to tread in them. May the Lord deliver us from those paths and their like.

And now I will begin describing my treatise.

**IV**

**21.**   Let the discerning student know that our intent in this treatise is to explain that in which we believe relating to this fundamental principle concerning which controversy arose among the scholars, and that is the resurrection of the dead. This treatise contains nothing new or additional to that which we have already said in our *Commentary on the Mishnah*[170] and the *Mishneh Torah*;[171] rather it contains a repetition of subjects and general lengthening (of discussion) and expansion of explanations so that even women[172] and the uneducated[173] can understand it; and no more.[174]

And I say that the resurrection of the dead which is widely known and accepted among our people, and which is acknowledged by all branches (of our nation), and which is often cited in prayers and in legends and in supplications composed by the prophets and the greatest of our Sages, and which are found throughout the Talmud and homiletical commentaries on Scripture, means[175] that the soul will return to its body after its separation. This is a premise about which there is no disagreement among the nation and this (matter) requires no interpretation. It is not permissible for any religious Jew to support[176] a man who believes the opposite.

**22.**   I will presently explain in this treatise why these Scriptural passages[177] are not interpreted allegorically[178] as we interpret many other passages in the Torah which we understand in other than the literal sense. Thus, the resurrection of the dead, which is the return of the soul to the body after death, has been mentioned by Daniel in such a way that it cannot be interpreted allegorically. For he said:[179] *And many[180] of them that sleep in the dust of the earth shall awake, some to everlasting life, and some to reproaches and everlasting abhorrence.* And the angel said to him:[181] *As for you, go thy way till the end be, and thou shalt rest, and shalt stand up to thy lot, at the end of the days.*

**23.**   Verily, that which is asserted about us that we said that the Scriptural passages about the resurrection of the dead are allegorical, is a widespread falsehood and a totally revolting statement on the part of the one who asserted it. Our writings are already widely disseminated, — let the reader show us where we even said such a thing! Perhaps (we were misunderstood) in what we said in relation to that which the Sages of Israel had already stated about the (resurrected) dead (bones) in (the book of) Ezekiel[182] concerning which there is a difference of opinion among the Sages of the Talmud.[183] For concerning everything where there is a difference of opinion but which does not lead to the performance of a Divine precept,[184] one can decide like either one of the two discussants. We have already mentioned this several times in the *Commentary on the Mishnah*. It is also apparent to us from those (Talmudic) statements that those individuals whose souls return to their bodies (after death) will eat and drink and engage in sexual intercourse and sire children and die[185] after an extremely long life like the life which will exist during the days of the Messiah.[186]

**24.** Further, the life following which there is no death, is the life in the world to come because there are no (physical) bodies there.[187] We firmly believe — and this is the truth which every intelligent person accepts — that in the world to come souls without bodies will exist like angels. The explanation is as follows: the body contains organs which serve the activities[188] of the soul as we have already decisively explained.[189] Everything that is in the body can be divided into three parts. There are organs through which food is assimilated[190] such as the mouth, the stomach, the liver, the intestines and all that which is in the lower abdomen. And there are organs through which procreation is achieved and they are the sexual organs, the procreative seed and the birth-bearing organ.[191] And there are organs through which body activities are regulated[192] so that it provides itself with all its needs, such as the eyes and the other sense organs, the blood vessels, the nerves and the sinews[193] through which all movements (of the body) are effectuated. Were it not for these, it would not be possible for a living being to move in quest of his food and to seek it and to flee from danger[194] which can destroy him and which can diminish his essence.[195]

And because food is not (always) edible without skills that man applies and without many preparations which require thought and intellect, man was endowed with the power of intellect with which to manage[196] these skills. Man is also endowed with natural organs with which to perform those skills, that is to say the hands and the feet, because the feet are organs which are not only used for walking.[197] The details of this principle are well known to the experts in that science.[198]

**25.**   Verily, we have already[199] explained that the existence of the entire body is for a single goal and that is to receive nutrition for the maintenance[200] of the body and for the bearing of children in the likeness (of the parents) in order to maintain the human race.[201] And when that goal is removed because there is no longer a need therefor, that is to say in the world to come — and this has already been explained to us by many of our Sages,[202] that "there is no eating or drinking or sexual intercourse there"[203] — it is clear that the body will not exist.

For the Lord, blessed be He, would not let anything exist without a purpose and would not create anything except for a reason. God forbid that His perfect actions be compared to the actions of idol worshippers: *they have eyes but they see not, they have ears but they hear not.*[204] So is God, may He be exalted, in the opinion of those (misbelievers),[205] in that He creates bodies, that is to say, organs which do not at all serve the purpose for which they were created, nor serve any other purpose. Perhaps to those (misbelievers), the people in the world to come do not have organs but nevertheless have physical bodies; or perhaps they are hard balls or columns or cubes. Such suggestions are really ludicrous: *Oh that ye would altogether hold your peace, and it would be your wisdom.*[206]

**26.**   The reason for all this[207] is as we have explained (elsewhere)[208] that the multitude of people do not conceive existence unless in connection with a body or that which is found within a body; and that which is not a body nor a property[209] of the body has for them no existence.[210] Whenever they wish to strengthen the existence of a certain matter, they add (physical) substance to it, that is to say that they overemphasize the essence of its substance. We have already clearly mentioned the fundamental principle in this regard[211] in the *Guide for the Perplexed*.[212] Whoever wishes to consider our opinion to be a blemish[213] is free to do as he pleases. And if someone wishes to consider our opinion to be in error and mistaken,[214] let him so state and we will not be annoyed thereby.

We are quite content — as we explained in the *Guide for the Perplexed*[215] — if only an intelligent person follows our view concerning belief in the truth, even if it be (only) a single individual, even if thousands of fools place us at a distance by believing in nonsense.

## V

**27.** Verily, we vehemently deny and we cleanse ourselves before Almighty God of the (accusation attributed to us that we espouse the) treatise that the soul will never return to the body and that it is impossible for that to occur. For such a denial (in the resurrection of the dead) leads to the denial of all miracles (chronicled in the Bible) and the denial of miracles is equivalent to denying the existence of God and abandonment of our faith. For we do consider the resurrection of the dead to be a cardinal principle of the Torah. There is nothing in our writings which would indicate a contradiction to the return of the soul to the body; on the contrary, (our writings) show the opposite. But he who wishes and chooses to speak slanderously about us and to attribute to us an opinion in which we do not believe, — just as those who are innocent of transgressions are (falsely) suspected, — and explains our words in a totally perverted manner[216] so that he makes us appear guilty[217] — he will ultimately be judged (by God) and his sentence will be the same as that of any wicked man who (falsely) suspects the innocent.[218]

**28.** After all the explanations (throughout our writings), it is not possible that a person should be misled and state that we believe that all Scriptural references to the resurrection of the dead are allegories, because some of them are to be understood literally as we have mentioned,[219] whereas others are undoubtedly allegorical,[220] whereas in regard to yet others there is doubt whether they are to be understood literally or allegorically.[221] And if you examine all the statements made by the Andalusian Sages[222] and commentators[223] concerning such Scriptural references and those (phrases) which precede and which follow them, the matter will become clear to you.[224]

According to the intent of this treatise, we have no need of this detail[225] because the truth of these matters is not increased by a reiteration of their words or by their frequent repetition nor are the truths diminished if they are not reiterated nor repeated. You (obviously) know that the (Scriptural) citation of the fundamental principle of the unity of God; namely, *the Lord is One*,[226] is not repeated in the Torah.[227]

**29.** Since we find that the words of the prophet[228] cannot bear any meaning (but the literal one) in that it states that the soul will return to the body, the definiteness of this prophetic narrative becomes established.[229] The truth of this narrative is not increased if one were to posit that every time the word resurrection occurs in Scriptures it means the return of the soul to the body; nor would the truth of this narrative be diminished if one assumes that some or all (of the Scriptural references to resurrection) except one phrase[230] are allegories.

In the final analysis, the prophetic narrative is met with once or twice,[231] and the ancient and modern Sages of Israel mention it innumerable times, and it has become widely known among our people and accepted by them, that the soul of a person returns to the body. This is the accepted context of the resurrection of the body wherever it is[232] mentioned by a scholar or an author.

# VI

**30.** Some people have raised doubts about our words at the end of our *Composition*[233] where we state the following: "Do not think that the King Messiah will have to perform signs and wonders, bring anything new into being, resurrect the dead or do similar things." We cited evidence for this assertion in our explanation.[234] Some people with weak intellects think that this assertion represents a denial in the resurrection of the dead and that it contradicts what we explained in the *Commentary on the Mishnah*[235] that "the resurrection of the dead is a cardinal principle of the Torah." This matter is all very clear, there is no doubt about it nor any contradiction. That which we asserted that the Messiah will not be required to perform a miracle such as splitting the sea or resurrecting a dead person in a miraculous way means that a miracle will not be asked of him since the prophets whose prophecies have been verified[236] have foretold his advent.[237]

It does not follow from this treatise that the Almighty, at the time of His choice, will not resurrect those He wishes to resurrect, whether during the era of the Messiah or before him or after his death. In the final analysis, there is nothing in our words in our *Composition*[238] which could raise doubts (about resurrection) in the minds of discerning people, — only to people with weak intellects.[239]

**31.** They have also raised doubts about our assertion[240] that "the words of Isaiah[241] *And the wolf shall dwell with the lamb . . . (and the lion shall eat straw)* are to be understood allegorically." We are not the only ones who have so stated; we have been preceded in the understanding of this subject by intelligent commentators such as Rabbi Moses Ibn Gekatila,[242] Ibn Balam[243] and other commentators.[244] The conclusion of the subject corroborates our view in that he states:[245] *They shall not hurt nor destroy in all My holy mountain, for the earth shall be full of the knowledge of the Lord,* etc. Here the reason given is that they will no longer destroy nor injure because they shall know the Lord. Can you, the congregation of Israel, find an intelligent person who would conceive a change in the lion who during our own times devours[246] and tears and then[247] repents and knows what he needs to know of his Creator, and knows that he should not injure, and repent and eat straw? If so, the following Scriptural phrase would be fulfilled:[248] *And the vision of all this is become unto you as the words of a sealed book,* etc.[249]

But we have already explained this subject in one of the chapters of our book *Guide For the Perplexed*.[250] And in our *Composition*[251] we clearly proved our thesis from the Sages' statement that the Messianic era will not differ from the order of creation.[252]

**32.**   Know that when we state that these assurances[253] and their like are to be understood allegorically, our words are not a decree, for a prophetic communication from the Almighty did not come to us telling us that it is an allegory, nor did we receive a tradition through the Sages from the prophets that they explain some parts of these matters allegorically. I will explain to you that which brought me[254] to this approach, and that is that our aim and the aim of every intelligent person among the very few is opposite to the aim of the multitude of people. For the most cherished and beloved thing to the multitude of Torah-observant people,[255] because of their ignorance, is to consider the Torah and human intellect to be two opposite poles.[256] Everything which is incomprehensible to their intellect[257] they consider to be a miracle. They flee from explaining something as a natural phenomenon whether it pertains to something recorded in the past, or in regard to something which is discernible at the present time, or whether it relates to something which is written will happen in the future. We, on the other hand, strive to reconcile the Torah with human intellect and regard everything in its natural light wherever possible, unless it is self-evident therefrom that it is of miraculous connotation and cannot be interpreted at all;[258] then we are forced to say that it is a miracle.

**33.**   In the *Guide For the Perplexed*[259] we have explained the clear language of Scriptures and the language used by the Sages, of blessed memory, as well as the many parables found in the words of the prophets.[260] We explained this matter at great length[261] to the point that it is impossible for any ignoramus to haughtily contradict it. For this reason, we and some of the prominent commentators who preceded us assert that these are parables, as we have explained.[262] It is also possible to state that when the world's population increases and the land becomes very fertile, injury of animals (to each other) will decrease in that they will live in har-

mony[263] with each other. Aristotle has already made this sugges-
tion in his book *On Animals*[264] where he gives this reason for the
infrequency of animals injuring each other in Egypt. It[265] may also
be an exaggeration as the Sages, of blessed memory, said "the
Torah speaks in the language of exaggeration."[266]

**34.** Even if it[265] is to be taken literally, it would be a miracle
exhibited solely on the Temple Mount as it is written:[267] *in all My
holy mountain.*[268] This situation is similar to the Rabbinic assertion:[269] "no snake or scorpion ever injured anyone in Jerusalem."
In the final analysis, these are all things which are not cardinal
principles of the Torah and one need not be overly concerned as to
how things will be (in the world to come).[270] A person must wait
for (clarification of) the essence of our faith in regard to these matters until they become speedily[271] fulfilled.[272] Then it will be clear
whether they are allegorical or miraculous.[273]

It is well known that we are very opposed[274] to changing the
order of creation.[275] Let those who precede or follow us who are
mistaken remain mistaken in that they cannot differentiate
between miraculous events which do not endure and which are not
permanent but occur as a temporary necessity[276] or to accredit a
prophet[277] — and natural events which always recur and which
represent the laws of nature[278] which the Sages of blessed memory
explained by repeatedly stating "the world follows the laws of
nature."[279] They also said: "no proof can be brought from miraculous events."[280] And Solomon said:[281] *For whatsoever God doeth
shall be forever; nothing can be added to it nor anything taken from
it.* It is thus clear that natural events always follow natural laws,
and we have also explained this matter in the *Guide for the Perplexed*[282] when we spoke of the inception of the world.

## VII

**35.** It seems to me[283] that that which led these people to be mistaken and to doubt our pronouncements about the resurrection of
the dead is the fact that we described the world to come at great
lengths[284] by explaining verified treatises[285] and citing all the state-

ments of the prophets and the Sages which pertain thereto. When, however, we discussed the resurrection of the dead, we did so in few words and merely said that the resurrection of the dead is a cardinal principle of our faith.[286] There are two reasons for this (lengthy discussion of the world to come and brief mention of the resurrection of the dead). The first is that all our compositions are concise and pure.[287] Our intent is not to expand on the body of the books and not to waste time with material that does not bring any benefit. Therefore, when we comment (on a subject),[288] we only comment on that which needs to be elucidated and only (briefly but) sufficient to make it understood. And when we write,[289] we write about subjects in a concise manner.

**36.** The second reason is that descanting should only be used to portray an obscure[290] subject so that its features are completely elucidated or when bringing proof to the truth of that subject. This approach is needed for three types of wisdom; namely, didactic sciences,[291] natural sciences,[292] and theological sciences.[293] For often times a subject in these (sciences) is obscure and its understanding is difficult[294] until all its aspects have been adequately explained. Many times the subject to be elucidated requires numerous proofs for the verification of the truth of the subject whose truth one is seeking to establish.

On the other hand, a miraculous event[295] is not obscure[296] nor difficult (to comprehend). It is impossible to bring proof to verify the truth of that (miracle) which has already occurred or that which we are (Divinely) promised will come to pass; rather we perceive it with our senses or accept it (as fact) from one who personally witnessed it. It is for this reason that we commented (at length) about the world to come and explained it to those who find it obscure and to show that this matter (of the world to come) is part of the natural course of events, that is to say, the immortality of the soul.[297]

**37.** On the other hand, the resurrection of the dead is one of the miracles and is absolutely explicit. This matter is (clearly) understood and needs only that we believe in it[298] as we cited in the true narrative.[299] It is a matter outside the laws of nature and one cannot prove it in a speculative manner. Indeed, miracles do occur and are all accepted (by us) through tradition and there is no other way.[300] What, therefore, could we say further about it and why (should we discuss it) at length? Do those who ask of us that we cite speculative proofs think that such proofs would make the resurrection of the dead an established fact?[301] There is no doubt that those people desire that I expound in my compositions on all the (Rabbinic) homiletical expositions and Talmudical narratives related to this subject. Such is more appropriate for people other than us according to the intent of what they write.[302]

You, the congregation of those who delve into our *Composition,*[303] already know that I always attempt to reduce controversy and polemics.[304] If it were possible for me to condense[305] the entire Talmud into one chapter, I would not condense it into two. How can I, therefore, be asked to cite all the homiletical expositions and narratives since they can be found in their places and can be read there? What benefit would accrue from repeating them and from saying that we composed them?

## VIII

And when we reached this point in this treatise — this was our ultimate goal[306] — we saw the total lack of utility (of expanding further on the subject of the resurrection of the dead) because such discussion would only contain repetitions of what we have already stated in the *Commentary on the Mishnah*[307] and in the *Composition*[308] and would (only) constitute additional explanations for those of small intellect and for those who tear down.[309] However, in order not to leave the subject totally without benefit of new information, we saw fit to discuss two appropriate matters[310] related to this subject. **38.** The first of these is to elucidate the subject of those Scriptural passages which are very numerous and which seem to clearly prove that resurrection of the dead is impossible. These (passages) seemingly cannot be interpreted (otherwise); for instance, it is written: *If a man die, may he live again?*[311] It is also written: *As the cloud is* *consumed and vanisheth away, so he that goeth down to the grave shall come up no more;*[312] and *Before I go whence I shall not return, even to the land of darkness and of the shadow of death;*[313] such phrases are numerous in the book of Job. And Hezekiah said: *They that go down into the pit cannot hope for Thy truth; the living, the living, he shall praise thee, as I do this day*[314] thus proving that *they that go down into the pit* are dead (forever). And it is also written: *For we must needs die, and are as water spilt on the ground which cannot be gathered up again.*[315] And it is written: *Wilt Thou work wonders for the dead? Or shall the shades arise and give Thee thanks? Selah.*[316] And it is written: *A wind passeth away, and cometh not again.*[317] If one delves into such Scriptural verses, one finds that they all totally negate the resurrection of the dead except for some literal interpretations[318] in Isaiah.[319] With a little reflection, it becomes clear that there is doubt as to whether such (a verse in Isaiah) is an allegory or is really true.[320] The following clearly-stated verses in Daniel are also responsible for the great confusion among the people: *And many of them that sleep in the dust of the earth shall awake,*[321] and *And thou shalt rest, and shalt stand up to thy lot, at the end of the days.*[322]

Some of these (Scriptural verses) have resulted in great doubts about this fundamental principle of the resurrection of the dead. Even some of those who (fully) believe in this fundamental principle have been forced to explain each of these aforementioned Scriptural verses (which negate resurrection) with extremely far-fetched explanations in order to render them acceptable.

**39.**   The second question relates to the fact that the Torah[323] does not mention this fundamental principle at all, either in the form of an allusion and certainly not explicitly. If one thinks that it is impossible that the Torah should not cite even allusions to this fundamental principle, — and when the Sages quote verses when they ask "How do we know that the resurrection of the dead is based on the Torah?,"[324] their intent is to show that these are hidden allusions — and all the more so because the Sages differ among these (verses),[325] then this second question would be: why is this subject not mentioned explicitly and with such clarity that no interpretation would be needed?[326] Rather, according to the person who thinks, it seems like the citation of a person who states something cryptically because he wishes to conceal it.

**40.** In response to the first question,[327] I hereby state that the words of the prophets and the language of the (Holy) books are narratives describing the existence of nature in its usual manner. It is well known that nature as it exists includes the union of the females of living beings with their males and the birth of like offspring, and the gradual growth of the offspring[328] until that living being[329] dies. It is not part of nature that that being return and exist again after its death. However, it is part of nature that when living beings die, those beings never return; rather they die and slowly dissolve until they disintegrate[330] into the elements and the original substance from which they came, so that not even a limited part is recognizable as part of (the dead) about which it could be said: this was such and such.[331]

Man alone is endowed with a measure of Godliness[332] and, therefore, of necessity, (this) part of him remains and does not perish nor become lost. However, the body of man perishes like all other living beings. A person who searches vigorously into these deep matters can also provide evidence from searching proofs on this subject, that is to say the immortality of the soul.[333] This is something which is part of nature and this is what the books of prophecy call the soul or the spirit in partnership with God. And the perishing of the body and its return to the elements from which that species was formed is as stated[334] in Scriptures: *And the dust returneth to the earth as it was, and the spirit returneth unto God who gave it.*[335] This is the law of nature.[336]

**41.** All these Scriptural verses must be understood in this manner. There is no difference between the verse[337] *If a man die, may he live again?*[338] and the verse *Shall we draw water for you from this rock?*[339] because neither is part of nature and is in fact impossible by natural means.[340] Rather the water issued out of the rock through a miracle. So, too, the resurrection of the dead is one of the (Divine) miracles. And there is no difference between the verse *Can the Ethiopian change his skin?*[341] and the verse *Wilt Thou work* *wonders for the dead?*[342] And the appearance of a pure hand once (miraculously) became white.[343]

And if a person should assert that it is impossible for an inanimate object to move, he would be speaking the truth according to the laws of nature, and this assertion would not be invalidated[344] by the changing of the stick into a serpent[345] because that was a miracle. Similarly, all the (Scriptural verses) which seem to be in opposition to the (doctrine of the) return of the dead refer to natural means, but such (verses) do not contradict the return of the dead if the Almighty wishes them to return. Thus, the contents of all these Scriptural verses should be elucidated for you as much as possible in a logical manner[346] and there is no need for you to interpret any of them with the distorted, far-fetched, unacceptable interpretations used by those who support their views in opposition to the (doctrine of the) resurrection of the dead and who strengthen their statements thereby.

**42.** Know that the denial of the return of the soul to the body is based on one of two reasons: either the denier rejects (the resurrection of the dead) because it is not a natural phenomenon and, according to this reason, he is forced to deny also all the miracles since they are unnatural phenomena; or he rejects (resurrection) because it is not (explicitly) stated in a Scriptural verse and he does not recognize the true narratives of the miraculous events. We have already explained that there are Scriptural verses, albeit few, which prove the return of the dead.[347] And if he asserts that we should interpret those verses as we interpret others,[348] we would say to him: that which forces you to explain (these verses allegorically) is the fact that the return of the dead is not natural and, therefore, you interpret these Scriptural verses so that they coincide with natural phenomena; similarly you are required to explain the conversion of the stick to a serpent and the descent of the manna and the standing (of the Jews) at Mt. Sinai[349] and the pillar of fire and cloud;[350] all these you are forced to interpret in a way that they coincide with natural phenomena. But we have already explained in the *Guide for the Perplexed*[351] when we discussed the inception[352] of the world that if one believes in the creation *ex* *nihilo*[352] of the world one is of necessity forced to believe that all the miracles (in the Torah) are possible, and among these is the possibility of the resurrection of the dead. Therefore, we believe in every possible occurrence, if it is related to us by a prophet,[353] and we do not find it necessary to interpret it (allegorically) nor to remove it from its literal meaning.

**43.** Nevertheless, certain things whose literal meanings are impossible such as the corporeality of God[354] must be interpreted (allegorically). However, that which is possible remains as is.[355] He who strives to explain the resurrection of the dead in such a way that the soul does not return to the body[356] does so because he believes that it is inconceivable to the human intellect and is not part of the laws of nature.[357] He is forced to the same conclusion in regard to all the other miracles (cited in Scriptures). All this, how-ever, is totally impossible according to the belief in the eternity[358] of the world.[359] He who believes in this antiquity is not at all con-sidered to be part of the congregation of Moses and of Abraham as we have explained in the *Guide for the Perplexed*.[360] We believe in these fundamental principles[361] and consider among them the resurrection of the dead in its literal meaning which we accept as a basic tenet of the Torah. And we say that it is not proper to inter-pret (allegorically) the two explicit Scriptural verses[362] which pro-vide clear evidence thereto[363] and which cannot support any (alle-gorical) interpretation.

## IX

**44.** Now, in regard to the answer to the second question, that is to say, why is the resurrection of the dead not mentioned in the Torah, the answer is as I will proceed to state: Know that it is widely appreciated and accepted that the whole Torah (to which we adhere) was not conceived by Moses our Teacher;[364] rather it is entirely from the Almighty.[365] We are, therefore, faced with the need to explore the question in intelligent ways[366] in that God commented to us (in His Torah) about life in the world to come[367] but did not explain the resurrection of the dead to us at all. The reason for this is that the resurrection of the dead will indeed occur as a miraculous event[368] as we have explained, and the credibility of such an event can only be based on the words of the prophet. At that time[369] (nearly) all of mankind belonged to the sect of Sabeans[370] who believed in the eternity of the world[371] and who considered the Almighty to be the spirit of the planets[372] as we have explained in the *Guide for the Perplexed*.[373] And they deny the transmission of prophecy from God to mankind.

**45.**    According to their belief, they are forced to deny (the verity of) miracles and attribute them to sorcery and cunning. Thus we perceive them[374] attempting to belie[375] the miracles[376] of Moses our Teacher of blessed memory with their enchantments: *For they cast down every man his rod*.[377] We also perceive how the (Israelites) themselves wondered: *We have seen this day that God doth speak with man, and he liveth*[378] showing that prophecy[379] was something they thought impossible. How then could the Torah describe a basic tenet[380] which requires belief in (the words of) a prophet to someone to whom the whole concept of prophecy is unacceptable?[381] They who believe in the eternity of the world also totally reject this (basic tenet). Were in not for (our belief) in miracles,[382] we would not be able to consider resurrection of the dead as a possible occurrence.

**46.** And when Almighty God wished to give the Torah to mankind[383] and to make known through the prophets[383a] His positive and negative commandments[384] throughout the world, as it is written: *And that My name may be declared throughout all the earth*,[385] — He produced the great miracles recorded throughout the Torah[386] to authenticate thereby the prophecy of the prophets[387] and the creation of the world. For a true miracle is clear proof of the creation of the world as we have explained in the *Guide for the Perplexed*.[388] And He did not exclude them[389] from the matters relating to this world such as reward and punishment, and from natural phenomena such as the immortality of the soul or its perdition, as we have mentioned, that is to say the world to come, and *kareth*.[390] Other than that, He cites nothing more (in the Torah) about resurrection.[391]

The matter continued this way until this basic tenet became accepted[392] and verified after the passage of generations. And there remained no doubt about the (truth of) the prophecies of the prophets nor about the occurrence of miracles. After that,[393] the prophets[394] narrated to us that which they were told by the Almighty concerning the resurrection of the dead and it became easy to accept it.[395]

**47.** And one finds that the Almighty[396] Himself took such an approach with the Israelites. He said to them: *And God led them not by the way of the land of the Philistines, although that was near; for God said, lest peradventure, the people repent when they see war, and they return to Egypt.*[397] Just as He gradually acclimatized them to matters of the world for fear lest they return to Egypt and the Divine plan for them[398] become nullified, so, too, He further feared that they would not accept this tenet, that is to say, resurrection, and the intended goal for them[398] in this regard would also be nullified. How could they, therefore, not be also gradually acclimatized to beliefs (in the tenets of Judaism)? And their leader[399] and their acclimatizer[400] is one (and the same).

And it is well known that those people to whom the Almighty[401] wished to have the Torah understood in their time adopted erroneous[402] ideas. It was said of them[403] at the end of the forty years (of desert wandering) after they had seen all the miraculous acts of God: *But the Lord hath not given you an heart to know, and eyes to see, and ears to hear, unto this day.*[404] And God, may He be blessed, knew that if He would tell them about the tenet of the resurrection of the dead, it would be strange to them and extremely difficult to accept. And they also made light of transgressions since the punishment therefor would not occur until much later. And, therefore, He frightened them and assured them of both good and bad which would occur speedily: *if thou shalt hearken* (you will be speedily rewarded); *if thou shalt not hearken* (you will be speedily punished);[405] and because of this, it[406] was easier to accept and more beneficial.[407] This, too, is of great benefit, that is to say listening (to God's commandments) improves one's worldly matters[408] and disobedience[409] makes them perish.[410]

**48.** It is already mentioned in the Torah that it is a permanent sign, that is to say the improvement of things (for Jews) by serving (the Lord) and their loss by disobedience. He said: *And they shall be upon thee for a sign and for a wonder, and upon thy seed forever.*[411] For this reason, the Sages said: "Israel is not under the influence of the constellations,"[412] that is to say, their success or their failure[413] is not governed by natural causes nor by happenstance but is dependent upon serving or disobeying (the Lord). And this sign is greater than any other sign.[414] And we have already explained that this (sign) applies to the judgment (by God) of the congregation (of Israel as a whole) as well as the judgment of an individual (Jew) as can be clearly seen from that story.[415] It is thus appropriate to state: *and upon thy seed forever.*[416] Also appropriate is the widely known saying among the nation: "If a person sees afflictions coming upon him, let him scrutinize his deeds."[417] The same idea is intended in the Scriptural passage describing the uniqueness of the nation: *which*[418] *the Lord thy God hath allotted to unto all the peoples . . . But the Lord hath taken you.*[419] This (passage) means that their destiny[420] does not follow the same course as that of all other nations; rather through this great miracle, God made them unique in that their actions are always responsible for[421] their success or their failure.[422]

# X

**49.** And that which now (at the conclusion of our treatise) remains for us to elucidate — even though it is more important than all which has been said above[423] — is that miracles are sometimes outside the realm of nature, such as the conversion of the rod (of Moses) to a serpent and the opening[424] of the earth (which swallowed) Korach and his followers[425] and the splitting of the (Red) sea. Other times, miracles occur in manners that are consistent with the laws of nature such as (the plagues of) locusts and hail and pestilence in Egypt. It is common that these types of occurrences happen at certain times and in certain places[426] such as the rending of the altar of Jeroboam at the bidding of the man of

God[427]: *This is the sign which the Lord hath spoken: Behold, the altar shall be rent, and the ashes that are upon it shall be poured out,*[428] for it is not unusual that a building may split, especially when newly constructed. Similarly the inundating rains that fell at the time of the harvest through (the prayer of) Samuel,[429] and the blessings and the curses which are mentioned in the Torah[430] — for each of these events can occur in any country and at any time, and these are all within the realm of possibility if one contemplates thereon.

**50.** However, these incidents which are within the realm of possibility are in fact miracles because (they fulfill) one or all three of the following conditions. The first of these is that the event occurred at precisely the time stated by the prophet as it happened in the case of Samuel: *I will call unto the Lord that He may send thunder and rain . . . so Samuel called unto the Lord, and the Lord sent thunder and rain that day,*[431] and as happened to the man of God who came from Judah: *The altar also was rent and the ashes poured out from the altar according to the sign which the man of God had given.*[432] The second condition is that the event occurred as an extremely rare type of occurrence such as the case of the locusts (where it states): *before them there were no such locusts as they, neither after them shall be such,*[433] and the hail where it states: *such as had not been in all the land of Egypt since it became a nation,*[434] and the pestilence where it states: *but of the cattle of the children of Israel there died not one,*[435] because the event occurred only in relation to a specific nation[436] or a specific place[437] or a specific severity,[438] all of which are extremely unusual, although possible. The third condition is the protraction and renewal and constancy of that event such as the blessings and the curses.[439] For if they occurred only once or twice, it would not have been (thought of as) a miracle and would have been considered as a chance occurrence. This matter has already been elucidated in the Torah[440] where it is written: *And if ye walk contrary unto Me, and will not hearken unto Me,* that is to say if you assume that an affliction which befalls you is a chance occurrence and not (Divine) punishment (for disobedience), the Almighty states that He will protract that suffering because of His burning anger in that you considered it as a chance occurrence,[441] and it is written: *And if ye walk contrary unto Me, then I will walk contrary unto you in fury.*[442]

**51.** After we have explained all this, know that a miracle that occurs outside the realm of nature[443] is not at all protracted and is not prolonged and does not persist unchanged. For were it to become permanent, it would lead to doubt concerning (the genuineness of) that miracle; had the staff remained a snake, one might suggest that it was a snake from the beginning.[444] For this reason, the miracle was proven genuine[445] when it reverted to being a staff: *and it become a rod in his hand.*[446] Similarly, if the opening[447] of the earth (which swallowed) Korach and his followers had remained open permanently, the miracle would have been incomplete;[448] its completion occurred when the earth returned to it earlier state: *and the earth closed upon them.*[449] The same (applies to the splitting of the Red Sea); *and the sea returned to its strength when the morning appeared, and the Egyptians fled against it.*[450]

It is because of this fundamental principle which I have elucidated that I do not believe[451] in the permanence of an occurrence which is outside of nature[452] as we have explained in this treatise. On the other hand, concerning a miracle which occurs through natural means, the more permanent it becomes and the longer it lasts, the more likely it is to be a miracle. For this reason, we believe that the permanence of the blessings and the curses,[453] — blessings for serving (the Lord) and curses if Israel constantly disobeys (the Lord) — proves that they are a sign and a miracle as we explained.[454]

**52.** Someone may ask: why was this miracle shown to them[455] rather than the ultimate miracle, that is to say, the resurrection of the dead and reward and punishment after death to the soul and the body?[456] This question would be equivalent to asking: why did (Moses), the servant[457] of God, effect a miracle by having the staff change into a snake rather than change a stone into a lion? This whole matter is dependent upon Divine wisdom[458] of which we don't understand even a small amount, especially in view of the fact that we have already discussed the classification of this wisdom.[459] Perhaps, there is a reason[460] or there are many other reasons which dictate Divine wisdom to act in this manner, but we cannot fathom them.

**53.**    And it is not appropriate for any intelligent person to criticize us for repeating a single topic many times in this treatise[461] or for the length of the explanation of this topic which doesn't require lengthy explanations.[462] For I composed this treatise (solely) for the multitude of people who are in doubt about our clearly enunciated statements (in our other writings) and for those who criticize the brevity of our words in regard to the resurrection of the dead.[463] On the other hand, mere hints suffice for those who are completely wise. For them it is not necessary to repeat nor to provide lengthy explanations since brief summaries are adequate as we provided for all these profound subjects in the *Guide For The Perplexed* and in all our compositions[464] conforming to the teaching of our Sages of blessed memory:[465] "He said to him: explain it. The latter replied: a wise man needs no explanation. He said to him: repeat it. The latter replied: a wise man needs no repetition."

It is thus clear to you that words to the wise do not require repetition or elucidation — *give (a little) to a wise man and he will be yet wiser.*[466] On the other hand, the multitude of people require both things together: *precept by precept, precept by precept, line by line, line by line.*[467] And with all that they understand a little: *here a little, there a little.*[468] Indeed it is appropriate to speak to each group according to its ability.[469]

And may Almighty God, because of His kindness, help us to maintain uprighteousness in word and in deed[470] and save us from sin and from error. Amen, Amen.[471]

Completed is the *Treatise on the Resurrection of the Dead.*

## References and Notes

1. Genesis 21:33. These words were uttered by the Patriarch Abraham when he established his residence in Beer-Sheba. Maimonides uses the same words to introduce his *Commentary on the Mishnah* and each of the three major sections of his *Guide for the Perplexed.*

2. Proverbs 8:8.

3. *Ibidem* 8:9.

4. *Ibidem* 12:23.

5. Finkel's critical edition omits the words "ben Yehuda."

6. Literally: an introduction of introductions.

7. Literally: weak souls.

8. *I.e.,* Moses.

9. Literally: to remove from our souls.

10. Hebrew: *mishniyim* from *sheney* meaning two, *i.e.,* those who believe in two gods.

11. Deut. 6:4.

12. Rabbinowitz omits the word "Christians" but in a footnote points out that the Finkel version containing this word is correct.

13. *I.e.,* may God preserve us from such false and evil interpretation of Scripture.

14. Literally: flesh and blood.

15. Hebrew: *umah* meaning people or nation; alternate version is *emunah* meaning faith or religion. Finkel points out that in Judaism *umah* and *emunah* are inseparable. Thus, says Rabbinowitz, one speaks of a German Catholic or an Arabic Christian but there is no Jewish Catholic or Jewish Christian.

16. According to Rabbinowitz, it is the Maimonidean assertion that the soul remains alive in the world to come. See Maimonides' Introduction to his Commentary on *Chelek,* the tenth chapter of Tractate Sanhedrin.

17. Literally: people or nation.

18. The belief in the resurrection of the dead.

19. Literally: girded ourselves; alternate translation; strengthened ourselves.

20. Rabbinowitz states that Maimonides is referring to his *Commentary on the Mishnah* and his *Mishneh Torah.*

21. Rabbinowitz points out that Maimonides made a similar statement when he wrote to his disciple Ibn Aknin: "know that I did not compose this work to become aggrandized among the Jews nor that I be bestowed with glory. . . . I did all of this only for the honor of the Lord, may He be blessed."

22. To clear the path to Torah.

23. Rabbinowitz substitutes "to prepare" (Hebrew: *lehachin*) for "to make understandable" (Hebrew: *lehavin*).

24. Literally: brought near.

25. One is not permitted to accept recompense for teaching Torah as stated in the Talmud (Chagigah 7a and Nedarim 37a): "just as I (the Lord) taught you (Torah) gratuitously, so must you teach (Torah) gratuitously . . ." The Lord, however, rewards those who teach Torah.

26. Because our intent was to do His will.

27. Even if we didn't succeed.

28. Sanhedrin 106b. as it is written, *But the Lord looketh on the heart* (I Samuel 16:7).

29. Literally: the portrayal of this matter.

30. Literally: we hope.

31. Rabbinowitz asserts that the several sentences, from the words "we prepared ourselves" in the previous paragraph to the same words here, represent a parenthetical note and that Maimonides now returns to his earlier thought.

32. The enumeration and explanation of the commandments.

33. There is great need for me to explain and justify the truths of some of the fundamental principles of our faith.

34. Rabbinowitz omits the word "regarded."

35. Literally: may God live, meaning the life of God.

36. Hebrew: *kopher* meaning heretic, atheist, non-believer, denier.

37. Finkel has: "anyone who states the opposite."

38. Hebrew: *min* meaning heretic, sectarian, apostate, infidel.

39. Hebrew: *epikoros* meaning heretic, sceptic, atheist, agnostic.

40. Literally: many discourses. Finkel has: "many discourses of *Berachoth*" meaning allegorical or homiletical interpretations of Scriptures as found in the Talmud, tractate Berachoth.

41. Literally: have not seen.

42. Literally: who were totally lost.

43. Hebrew: *mazkinim*. Finkel cites another interpretation: were in doubt. Rabbinowitz has *muktzah* meaning set aside or untouchable.

44. Rabbinowitz has: "blind people."

45. Like his *Mishneh Torah*.

46. Like his *Guide for the Perplexed*.

47. Literally: roots.

48. Those who exclusively study Talmud but no other subjects.

49. Part I, Introduction, where Maimonides states ". . . it is not the purpose of this treatise to make its totality understandable to the vulgar or to beginners in speculation, nor to teach those who have not engaged in any study other than the science of the Torah . . ."

50. Rabbinowitz, citing Baneth, offers an alternate version: "so that at least these truths will be accepted by all."

51. See Rosner, F. (translator and editor). *Moses Maimonides' Commentary on the Mishnah*. New York, Feldheim, 1975. XV and 235 pp.

52. Literally: which should be believed.

53. Hebrew: *Rabban* referring to those Rabbis or teachers who believe in the oral law as opposed to heretics who only accept the written law (*i.e.,* Bible), literally. Finkel cites Shem Tob Palquera who interprets *Rabban* to refer to theologist.

54. The tenth chapter of Tractate Sanhedrin. See Rosner, F. (translator) *Moses Maimonides' Mishnah Commentary on Tractate Sanhedrin.* Sepher-Hermon, New York, 1981, 214 pp.

55. That He is One, and that He is the first and the last.

56. See Maimonides' thirteen basic principles of our faith in his *Mishnah Commentary on Sanhedrin.* See note 54.

57. Literally: of the Torah.

58. See the Laws of the Fundamental Principles of the Torah and the Laws of Repentance in volume I of Maimonides' famous *Mishneh Torah.* He often refers to his *Mishneh Torah* as his *Composition.*

59. Literally: good intellect.

60. Alternate version: of the words.

61. Alternate translation: of the Torah and the Talmud.

62. Hebrew: *talmidei chachamim.*

63. Hebrew: *chachamim.* Finkel omits this word.

64. Hebrew: *ga'onim.*

65. Literally: branches or paragraphs.

66. Literally: arranged in their mouths.

67. Rabbinowitz has: and their Talmudic learning should go up the path. Finkel points out that this phrase is reminiscent of Ta'anith 7b–8a where the Talmud states: if you see a student to whom his studies are as hard as iron, it is because he has failed to systematize his studies.

68. Both Talmudic (*i.e.,* Rabbinic) as well as Biblical tenets and ideations are based on the Torah. Rabbinowitz explains that Rabbinic enactments such as the laws of *erubin* (amalgamations of abodes to permit carrying in a common courtyard) which are based on the observance of the Sabbath (Exodus 16:29) as well as the kindling of lights on Chanukah which is based on the historical occurrence of miracles to the Jews are all Rabbinic commandments over which a blessing is uttered invoking God's name just as if these were Biblical commands because all Rabbinic decrees are rooted in and authorized by the Torah (Deut. 17:11).

69. The Torah scholars.

70. See the first precept in Maimonides' *Mishneh Torah, Hilchoth Yesodei Hatorah* 1:1.

71. Hebrew: *gavom,* literally: backs. See Isaiah 38:17 where the same word is used.

72. *I.e.,* physical pleasures and monetary riches.

73. *Mishneh Torah, Hilchoth Teshuvah,* Chapt. 8.

74. Cf. note 54.

75. See Sanhedrin 90b.

76. *I.e.,* very few people discuss the subject of the world to come.

77. In Maimonides' Introduction to *Chelek*.

78. Maimonides' *Mishneh Torah, Hilchoth Teshuvah* 8:1 cites Deut. 22:7 *that it may be well with thee, and that thou mayest prolong thy days,* which the Sages interpret (Kiddushin 39b) to refer to the world to come.

79. Hebrew: *kareth,* to be cut off.

80. *Hilchoth Teshuvah* 8:1 cites Numbers 15:31, *that soul shall be utterly cut off* which the Sages interpret (Sanhedrin 64b) to refer to the world to come.

81. *Mishneh Torah, Hilchoth Teshuvah,* Chapt. 8 and 9.

82. In the world to come. See Maimonides' Introduction to *Chelek.*

83. Finkel adds: of blessed memory.

84. *Mishneh Torah, Hilchoth Teshuvah* 3:6—14.

85. After enumerating individually those who have no share in the world to come, we cited them again as follows: "all these twenty-four classes of people which we enumerated, even if they are Israelites, have no portion in the world to come." (*opus.cit.* 3:14)

86. *Ibid.* 8:3.

87. See Maimonides' Introduction to *Chelek* and his *Mishneh Torah, Hilchoth Teshuvah* 8:2.

88. In Berachoth 17a, the text reads: no eating and no drinking and no procreation. In his Introduction to *Chelek,* Maimonides states: no eating, no drinking, and no washing and no anointing and no sexual intercourse. In his *Mishneh Torah* (see previous note) and later in his *Treatise on Resurrection* (*vide infra,* section #25), the wording is the same as here: no eating and no drinking and no sexual intercourse. Finkel therefore concludes that Maimonides did not here intend to cite the Talmud exactly.

89. See Shabbath 77b: "of all that God created in His world, He did not create anything for naught." See however Abodah Zarah 4:7. In his *Guide* (2:14) and in his *Introduction to the Mishnah* (see English edition by F. Rosner, Feldheim Publishers, New York 1975), Maimonides also states that God created nothing for naught on this world.

90. Hebrew: *peninim* meaning "substance" or "essence" but also "pearl" or "jewel."

91. Finkel states that Maimonides is referring to idle talk indulged in by women in a mourner's house. See also below section 17.

92. That there is no corporeal existence in the world to come.

93. Each did not eat or drink for 40 days and nights; Moses as in Exodus 34:28 and Elijah as in I Kings 19:8.

94. Lamentations 1:12.

95. Kiddushin 39b.

96. See Maimonides' *Guide* 1:46: "the organs of generation are the means of

preserving the species; the hands, the feet and the eyes are the means of improving the condition of man and bringing his actions to perfection . . ."

97. Who believe in corporeal existence in the world to come.

98. Literally: existence.

99. Physical parts of the body and the senses of touch, smell, hearing, etc.

100. Literally: occurrences; *i.e.,* qualities such as strength and weakness, miserliness and generosity, arrogance and humility, etc.

101. Isaiah 28:9. *i.e.,* these fools act like babies.

102. See also Maimonides' *Guide* 1:26.

103. Because the two are not comparable; if the substance is destroyed, it ceases to exist.

104. The physical body deteriorates but the spiritual soul has permanence. See Maimonides' *Mishneh Torah, Hilchoth Yesodei HaTorah* 1: 11–12.

105. See Maimonides' *Guide* 2:1.

106. *I.e.,* free of corporeality.

107. Alternate translation: minds. See Maimonides' Introduction to *Chelek.*

108. Part 1:49 and part 2:6 and 10.

109. Literally: angels are bodies.

110. Genesis 18:8.

111. *I.e.,* that angels and souls are corporeal.

112. For one who believes that God is corporeal is classified as a heretic (*Mishneh Torah, Hilchoth Teshuvah* 3:7).

113. Because no Biblical prohibition is involved. See Maimonides' *Commentary on the Mishnah,* Chagigah 2:1.

114. That angels and people in the world to come are corporeal.

115. Literally: places a blemish in our view.

116. Literally: substance.

117. Rabbinowitz has: his error.

118. Ordinary people embrace the world view of the corporeality of angels and life in the world to come because they cannot fathom pure spiritual life devoid of physical substance.

119. Literally: miracles.

120. See Maimonides' *Mishneh Torah, Hilchoth Yesodei HaTorah* 1:7–9.

121. Berachoth 31b.

122. See Maimonides' *Guide for the Perplexed* 1:26.

123. *I.e.,* angels and people.

124. Because the Torah mentions them.

125. Rabbinowitz suggests that Maimonides' reference here is to mysticism and to the "instantaneous" comprehension by mystics of matters which ordinarily require penetrating analysis and serious meditation.

126. Literally: received traditions.

127. Rabbinowitz omits the phrase "in many places in the Talmud."

128. Pesachim 119b; Chagigah 13a.

129. Rabbinowitz cites Baneth who states that the expression "may their memory be blessed" is an error and should be omitted.

130. Literally: until they know no place therefor. Alternate translation: to the point that they don't know any part thereof.

131. Section 1:33–35; Section 2:33 and 47; Section 3:50.

132. Literally: sufficient.

133. Hidden meanings of Torah.

134. *The Mishneh Torah.*

135. Literally: one of the disciples.

136. Literally: all the people of that place.

137. *Hilchoth Teshuvah* 8:2.

138. His colleagues.

139. Hebrew idiomatic expression *zeh batel bemiyuto* means that his opinion is nullified because so few agree with it.

140. Equivalent to the year 1189 of the Common Era or the year 4949 since the creation of the world. The Seleucid era used in documents began in 311–312 B.C.E. following the death of Alexander the Great in 323 B.C.E. and the many battles relating to succession to his throne.

141. Alternate translation: southern lands.

142. That they are only souls without bodies. See *Hilchoth Teshuvah* 8:2.

143. Sanhedrin 90a; Baba Bathra 16a; and elsewhere.

144. 2 Samuel 2:6; Daniel 12:2; and elsewhere.

145. Denial in the resurrection of the dead.

146. Belief in the resurrection of the dead.

147. Corresponding to 1191 C.E.

148. Among them Maimonides' famous disciple Joseph Ibn Aknin.

149. Resurrection of the dead and the world to come.

150. Rabbinowitz cites Baneth who substitutes "lived" for "was ordained."

151. He headed the Rabbinical College from 1163 to 1197 C.E.

152. Meaning unclear, perhaps he restricted his words of criticism. Rabbinowitz substitutes "he helped with" (Hebrew: *ozar*) for "he restricted" (Hebrew: *otzar*). Rabbinowitz also cites another variant reading: "he perverted."

153. Hebrew: *gaon* meaning genius but also the title of the heads of the Babylonian academies.

154. To support the truth of the resurrection of the dead. For example, there is the legend of a pious man overhearing two spirits speaking to each other (Berachoth 18b).

155. See note 91 above.

156. Literally: the speakers. Rabbinowitz states this expression refers to religious philosophers who believe in the Laws of Islam. See Maimonides' *Guide For the Perplexed* 1:71.

157. Rabbinowitz points out that Maimonides' view is that our belief in the resurrection of the dead is not based on logical deduction or speculation but on faith and belief in the Divine miracle of resurrection just as we believe in all the other miracles mentioned in holy writings.

158. Arabic physician and philosopher who lived from 980 to 1037 C.E. He is frequently cited by Maimonides, especially in his medical writings. See Brockelmann's *Geschichte der Arabischen Litteratur,* Vol. 1, p. 456.

159. Rabbinowitz asserts that this book was written by the apostate Abu al Birkat Hibat Allah whereas Finkel states that the author was the Jewish renegade Hibat Allah ibn Malkan (circa 1160–70) and refers the reader to Steinschneider's *Al Farabi.* St. Petersburg, 1869, p. 10, and his *Arabischer Litteratur,* pp. 182–6.

160. Rabbinowitz omits: in their entirety.

161. Literally: remaining of souls.

162. Alternate translation: the mind.

163. Meaning unclear: either they don't understand it or they deny a separate existence for the soul.

164. Based perhaps on the literal interpretation of Levit. 17:14.

165. Literally: an occurrence. *e.g.,* beauty, ugliness, strength, weakness, etc. none of which have independent existence.

166. Literally: the speakers. See note 156 above.

167. As do all body properties when the body dies.

168. Hebrew: *gaon.* See note 153 above. In many instances in this work, Maimonides follows the word *gaon* with the expression: May God watch over him.

169. Literally: permitted.

170. Introduction to chapter *Chelek.*

171. Literally: composition. See *Hilchoth Teshuvah* chapters 8 and 9.

172. Rabbinowitz points out that women in those days served primarily as housewives and mothers and did not study Torah.

173. Literally: ignorant or foolish people.

174. Rabbinowitz asserts that Maimonides here shows his annoyance at Rabbi Samuel Halevi by writing a treatise in which he, Maimonides, only repeats that which he has already written elsewhere, without adding anything new.

175. Literally: its context.

176. Literally: to believe in.

177. Which speak of the resurrection of the dead.

178. Literally: explained.

179. Daniel 12:2. Rabbinowitz erroneously has 11:2.

180. *Many* but not all since the resurrection of the dead is limited to the righteous (Genesis Rabbah 13).

181. Daniel 12:13.

182. Ezekiel Chapter 37.

183. Sanhedrin 92b. Maimonides decides like Rabbi Judah who says that the

story of the resurrection of the dry bones by Ezekiel was but a parable as opposed to Rabbi Eliezer who said that the dead whom Ezekiel resurrected stood up, uttered song and died, or Rabbi Eliezer, the son of Rabbi Yose the Galilean, who said that the dead whom Ezekiel revived went up to Palestine, married wives and begat sons and daughters.

184. Such as the dead of Ezekiel where the differences of opinion have no practical application since the Rabbis are arguing over an historical event, the correct nature of which cannot be proven.

185. As specifically affirmed by Rabbi Eliezer the son of Rabbi Yose the Galilean (Sanhedrin 92b).

186. Rabbinowitz explains that the extremely long life in the Messianic era can be attributed to the absence of cares and worries and anxieties coupled with the blessings of plenty and good life.

187. The Messianic era will see souls reunited with their bodies but in the world to come, there will be only spiritual existence. See *Hilchoth Yesodei Hatorah* 4: 3–4.

188. Alternate translation: properties.

189. See Maimonides' *Eight Chapters* (Edit. Joseph I. Gorfinkle. Columbia Univ. Press. 1912. Chapter 1–2) where he rejects the statement of Hippocrates that there are three souls, the physical, the vital and the psychical. Maimonides asserts that the human soul is one but it has diversified activities and five faculties: the nutritive (also known as the "growing" faculty), the sensitive, the imaginative, the appetitive, and the rational.

190. Literally: in which food is completed.

191. *I.e.,* the uterus.

192. Literally: body matters are corrected.

193. Ligaments and tendons.

194. Literally: that which is against him.

195. See Maimonides' *Guide for the Perplexed,* Section 1; Chapters 46 and 72.

196. Finkel points out that Ibn Tibbon, who translated Maimonides' *Treatise on Resurrection* from the original Arabic into Hebrew, erroneously translated this word to "remember" rather than "manage." Thus many of the Hebrew manuscripts perpetuate this error.

197. The feet can also be used to kick, to dig, etc. Rabbinowitz' version (erroneously) has: because the feet are organs only used for walking.

198. Biology, physiology, zoology.

199. Rabbinowitz omits the word "already."

200. Literally: permanence or continuity or perseverance.

201. Literally: to maintain that form of body.

202. Rabbinowitz omits "many of" but adds "of blessed memory." These are variations of the different manuscripts as cited by Finkel in the textual variants.

203. Berachoth 17a. See also note 88 above.

204. Psalms 115:5–6.

205. Who believe that physical bodies will exist in the world to come.

206. Job 13:5 has the third person whereas the original and the translation have the second person.

207. The error that misbelievers ascribe the existence of physical bodies in the world to come.

208. *Guide for the Perplexed.* Section 1, Chapter 26.

209. Literally: power.

210. Rabbinowitz adds: at all.

211. That only spiritual life is everlasting.

212. Section 1, Chapters 1, 26 and 46.

213. See note 115 above.

214. Rabbinowitz asserts that Maimonides is here alluding to Rabbi Samuel Halevi, who, in his treatise on resurrection to the Jews in Yemen, stated that some of Maimonides' statements concerning the resurrection of the dead were erroneous and mistaken.

215. Section 1, Introduction.

216. Literally: with a distant explanation.

217. Literally: he tips the scale to the guilty side.

218. In a footnote, Finkel refers the reader to Maimonides' *Commentary on Abot* ed. Baneth. Berlin 1905 p. 6, "He who (falsely) suspects the innocent will be smitten on his body" (Yoma 19b). See also Shabbath 97a.

219. *E.g.,* Daniel Chapter 12.

220. Rabbinowitz cites: *And the wolf shall dwell with the lamb* (Isaiah 11:6) as an example.

221. Rabbinowitz cites: *Thy dead shall live, my dead bodies shall arise* (Isaiah 26:19) as an example.

222. Spanish Rabbinical scholars.

223. Rabbinowitz omits: Commentators.

224. Whether the Scriptural phrase is to be interpreted literally or allegorically.

225. To know which phrase is to be interpreted literally and which allegorically.

226. Deut. 6:4.

227. Not even once more.

228. Chapter 12 in Daniel.

229. Rabbinowitz explains that prophetic words cannot, in Maimonides' opinion, be subject to analysis and dispute since prophecy supersedes logic and philosophy and must therefore be accepted literally.

230. Such as in Chapter 12 of Daniel.

231. Rabbinowitz substitutes: many times.

232. Literally: if it is. Rabbinowitz substitutes: even if it is not.

233. *Mishneh Torah, Hilchoth Melachim* 11:3.

234. Rabbinowitz quotes the Talmud (Berachoth 34b): there is no difference between this world and the time of the Messiah except for servitude to foreign powers (in this world).

235. Introduction to chapter *Chelek* in tractate Sanhedrin.

236. Such as Isaiah.

237. Literally: have designated him.

238. The *Mishneh Torah.*

239. Literally: disciples who are beginners.

240. *Hilchoth Melachim* 12:1.

241. Isaiah 11:6. Rabbinowitz erroneously cites Isaiah 11:19.

242. Rabbinowitz states that he was born in Cordoba in the year 1070 and was a disciple of Rabbi Jonah Ibn Ganach.

243. In a footnote, Finkel points out that Ibn Balam does not comment on the passage in his commentary on Isaiah (see *Gloses d'Abou Zakariya Yahia ben Bilam sur Isaie.* ed. Derenbourg, Paris, 1892, pp. 49–50.

244. See the commentaries of Ibn Ezra and *Radak* on Isaiah 11:6.

245. Isaiah 11:9.

246. Literally: revolts, rebels.

247. In the world to come.

248. Isaiah 29:11.

249. Just as the vision of Isaiah of the lamb eating with the wolf is not understood, so too, the concept of the resurrection of the dead is not understood by people of weak intellect.

250. Section 2, Chapter 29.

251. *Hilchoth Melachim* 12:1.

252. There is no difference between this world and the world to come except for servitude to foreign powers (in this world) (Berachoth 34b; Shabbath 63a and 151b).

253. That the wolf will eat with the lamb and the lion shall eat straw.

254. Rabbinowitz substitutes: us.

255. Literally: people of the Torah, i.e., religious Jews who believe in and observe the tenets of the Torah.

256. Literally: contradictory corners. See *Guide for the Perplexed,* Section 2, Chapters 22 and 23.

257. Literally: separate and set apart from the intellect.

258. Such as the verses in Chapter 12 of the book of Daniel which, within their context, cannot be interpreted allegorically nor intellectually in a natural light.

259. Section 1, Introduction.

260. The prophets often use parables and allegories, *e.g.,* Hosea 12:11 and Ezekiel 17:2.

261. We explained the reason for the frequent use of parables in Biblical and Rabbinic writings. Rabbinowitz cites King Solomon's Proverbs 1:6, *To understand a parable and a metaphor, the words of the Sages and their riddles,* which is interpreted (Song of Songs Rabbah 1:1:8) as follows: Until Solomon arose no one could properly understand the words of the Torah. . . . Imagine a deep well full of water, cold, sweet and wholesome water, but no one was able to get a drink of it, until one man came and joining rope to rope and cord to cord, drew from it and drank, and then all began to draw and drink. So proceeding from one thing to another, from one parable to another, Solomon penetrated to the innermost meaning of the Torah. . . .

262. *Hilchoth Melachim* 12:1 *"The wolf will live with the lamb* is a parable" meaning the wicked, who are compared to wolves, will live in harmony with the righteous.

263. Literally: closer.

264. See Aristotle's *History of Animals,* book 9, chapter 2.

265. The Scriptural phrase *and the wolf shall dwell with the lamb* and others like it.

266. Chullin 90b. For example: *Large and fortified cities go up to the heavens* (Deut. 1:28).

267. Isaiah 11:9.

268. Rabbinowitz points out that Maimonides, in his *Guide for the Perplexed* (Section 3, Chapter 11) considers this verse to be a parable or allegory.

269. Aboth 5:5 — Rabbinowitz erroneously cites Aboth 4:5.

270. Literally: how to believe in them.

271. Rabbinowitz has: speedily in our time.

272. *I.e.,* with the coming of the Messiah.

273. Maimonides is telling us to believe in the words of the prophets but not to delve into the details. We should believe in the coming of the Messiah, the resurrection of the dead and the world to come which he hopes we will all speedily experience. In the meantime there is no need to explain all the Scriptural phrases relating to these subjects although we attempt to understand them from their natural and not supernatural aspects.

274. Literally: we flee from.

275. *I.e.,* we prefer to interpret these matters as natural phenomena.

276. *E.g.,* the drying of the hand of Jeroboam ben Neboth. (I Kings 13:4) or the opening of the earth to swallow Korach and his followers (Numbers 16:30).

277. *E.g.,* the changing of Moses' staff into a serpent (Exodus 4:3).

278. Literally: the conduct of the world.

279. Finkel points out that in Abodah Zarah 54b, the phrase "the world follows the laws of nature" is found once and the phrase "the world follows the laws of nature and proceeds (in that way)" twice. The Munich Ms. (Vol. 11, f.383b) has the former phrase in all three cases as does the *Guide for the Perplexed* (Section 2

Chapter 29) and the *Thamaniyyat Fusul,* edit. Wolff, Leiden, 1903, p. 30.

280. Finkel points out that this quotation seems to be a synthesis of "no proof can be brought from miraculous events" (Berachoth 60a) and "no proof can be brought from a carob tree" (Baba Metzia 59b).

281. Ecclesiastes 3:14.

282. Section 2, Chapters 19, 25 and 29.

283. Rabbinowitz omits: to me.

284. In the *Commentary on the Mishnah* and the *Mishneh Torah.*

285. Unclear phrase. Rabbinowitz explains: philosophical matters.

286. Literally: true cornerstone.

287. Hebrew: *kav venaki*; literally: small quantity but well sifted.

288. Such as the *Commentary on the Mishnah.*

289. Literally: compose. *i.e.,* the *Mishneh Torah.*

290. Literally: hidden.

291. Such as mathematics.

292. Such as biology.

293. Such as metaphysics.

294. Literally: its portrayal is distant.

295. Rabbinowitz has: the words of those who perform miracles.

296. Literally: its portrayal is not hidden.

297. Rabbinowitz states that soul here refers to one's intellect which remains permanently after its separation from the body at the time of death, and that this is the course of nature. See *Hilchoth Yesodei HaTorah* 4:9 and *Guide for the Perplexed,* Section 1, Chapter 41.

298. Resurrection of the dead requires no lengthy explanations or commentary.

299. Chapter 12 in the book of Daniel which is to be understood literally, not allegorically.

300. We believe in miracles purely on faith without any attempts at "proving" them.

301. Literally: obligatory.

302. For descriptions of this and other categories of people Maimonides deplores, see his Commentary on *Chelek* in Tractate Sanhedrin.

303. The *Mishneh Torah.*

304. Rabbinowitz states that Maimonides here refers to his *Mishneh Torah* in which he provides only final adjudications without the background Talmudic differences of opinions and controversies among the Sages.

305. Literally: place.

306. We have explained why we did not write at length about the resurrection of the dead as we did about the world to come even though both are fundamental tenets of Judaism.

307. Introduction to chapter *Chelek.*

308. *Mishneh Torah, Hilchoth Teshuvah* 3:10–14.

309. Hebrew: *hores*, literally: to break through or to overthrow or to destroy. Finkel states that this word is the same as that used in Exodus 19:21 where it states: *lest they break through unto the Lord to gaze and many of them perish*, and that Maimonides here refers to a person who enters where he is not supposed to enter, or begins something before he is supposed to begin, or speaks when he is not supposed to speak, all without thinking or considering the consequences of such action.

310. Literally: questions.

311. Job 14:14.

312. *Ibid.* 7:9.

313. *Ibid.* 1:21. Rabbinowitz omits the second half of this sentence.

314. Isaiah 38:18–19.

315. II Samuel 14:14.

316. Psalms 88:11.

317. *Ibid.* 78:39.

318. Rabbinowitz has: some verses.

319. For example: *Thy dead shall live, my dead bodies shall arise, awake and sing ye that dwell in the dust* (Isaiah 26:19).

320. See the Biblical commentaries on Isaiah 26:19.

321. Daniel 12:2.

322. *Ibid.* 12:13.

323. The Pentateuch.

324. Sanhedrin 90b; 91b; 92a.

325. Each Sage cites a different Biblical verse as the hidden allusion to the resurrection of the dead.

326. Literally: cannot support interpretation.

327. How to explain and interpret the Scriptural verses which seem to negate the resurrection of the dead.

328. From infancy through adolescence, adulthood, middle age and old age.

329. Literally: man.

330. Literally: return to.

331. See *Hilchoth Yosodei HaTorah* 4:3.

332. Intellect or soul.

333. Literally: the remaining over of that which remains from that with which man was endowed.

334. Literally: brought.

335. Ecclesiastes 12:7.

336. Literally: this is what is in nature.

337. Literally: his saying.

338. Job 14:14.

339. Numbers 20:10.

340. Literally: restrained therein.

341. Jeremiah 13:23.

342. Psalms 88:11.

343. An allusion to the hand of Moses which suddenly became leprous (Exodus 4:6). See also *Guide for the Perplexed,* Section 2, Chapter 29.

344. Literally: belied.

345. Exodus 7:10.

346. Literally: from the truth. *i.e.,* use logic and intellect to interpret these verses, whenever possible.

347. Such as in Daniel 12:2 and 12:13.

348. *I.e.,* allegorically, not literally.

349. Exodus Chapter 19.

350. Exodus 13:21.

351. Section 2, Chapter 25.

352. Hebrew: *chidush,* literally: renewal.

353. As in Daniel 12:2 and 12:13.

354. See *Mishneh Torah, Hilchoth Yesodei HaTorah* 1:7.

355. Any miracle performed by the will of God is to be accepted literally.

356. He who agrees that a resurrection will take place but denies the reunion of the body and soul.

357. Rabbinowitz points out that the laws of nature can sometimes be changed through the will of God as the conversion of the stick to a serpent and the conversion of water to blood (the first plague visited upon the Pharaoh). In his *Commentary on the Mishnah* (Aboth 5:6), Maimonides states that all miracles were instituted in the nature of things at the time of the six days of creation. In his *Introduction to Aboth* (Eight Chapters, Chapter 8, see note 189 above), he states that "all miracles which deviate from the natural course of events, whether they have already occurred, or, according to promise, are to take place in the future, were fore-ordained by the Divine Will during the six days of creation, nature being then so constituted that those miracles which were to happen really did afterwards take place. Then, when such an occurrence happened at its proper time, it may have been regarded as an absolute innovation, whereas in reality it was not." Maimonides also supports this view in his *Guide for the Perplexed* (Section 2, Chapter 29) where he refers to Genesis Rabbah 5:4 and Exodus Rabbah 21:6 which state: "when God created the world, He made an agreement that the sea should divide, the fire not hurt, the lions not harm, the fish not swallow persons singled out by God for certain times, and thus the whole order of things changes whenever He finds it necessary."

358. Literally: antiquity.

359. Those, like Aristotle who say that the world came into being from *materia prima* which is eternal.

360. Section 2, Chapters 17, 23 and 25.

361. Belief in the creation of the world *ex nihilo* and belief in all the miracles cited in Scriptures.

362. Daniel 12:2 and 12:13.

363. To the literal acceptance of the verses which speak of the resurrection of the dead.

364. Literally: we do not believe that it is from the mouth of Moses our Teacher.

365. God transmitted the Torah to us through Moses.

366. *I.e.*, reverently.

367. Albeit not explicitly but clear enough. For example: *That it may be well with thee, and that thou mayest prolong thy days* (Deut. 22:7) is interpreted by the Sages (Kiddushin 39b) as the world to come; so too *that soul shall be utterly cut off* (Numbers 15:31) is also interpreted (Sanhedrin 64b) to refer to the world to come.

368. Not like the world to come which is a natural event.

369. When the Torah was given to the Israelites.

370. Rabbinowitz states that Maimonides includes in this term all the ancient peoples who were idol worshippers, especially those who idolized the stars and the planets.

371. Literally: antiquity. They deny the creation of the world *ex nihilo* by the Almighty.

372. *I.e.*, the force which moves the planets.

373. Section 1, Chapter 70; Section 3, Chapters 29 and 45. Rabbinowitz cites from Maimonides' *Guide* (I:70): The Sages stated (Chagigah 12a): "The high and exalted dwelleth on *arabot*" as it is written: *Extol Him that rideth upon arabot* (Psalms 68:4). How is it proved that heaven and *arabot* are identical? The one passage has *who rideth upon arabot*, the other *who rideth upon the heaven* (Deut. 33:26). Hence it is clear that in all these passages reference is made to the same all-surrounding sphere . . . Consider well that the expression "dwelling over it" is used by them, and not "dwelling in it." The latter expression would have implied that God occupies a place or is a power in the sphere, as was in fact believed by the Sabeans, who held that God was the soul of the sphere. By saying "dwelling over it," they indicated that God was separate from the sphere, and was not a power in it. Know also that the term "riding upon the heavens" has figuratively been applied to God in order to show the following excellent comparison. The rider is better than the animal upon which he rides—the comparative is only used for the sake of convenience, for the rider is not of the same class as the animal upon which he rides—furthermore, the rider moves the animal and leads it as he likes; it is as it were his instrument, which he uses according to his will; he is separate from it, apart from it, not connected with it.

374. The Egyptian sorcerers.

375. Literally: divide or separate.

376. Rabbinowitz has "miracle" in the singular, *i.e.,* the changing of the staff into a serpent.

377. Exodus 7:12.

378. Deut. 5:21.

379. God's revealing Himself to the Israelites at Mt. Sinai.

380. Literally: an item. *i.e.,* the resurrection of the dead.

381. Literally: unexplained.

382. Such as the creation of the world.

383. Finkel points out that the original Arabic phrase *an yishra Yisrael* became *Torah lebnei adam* in Hebrew translation probably due to censorship. Rabbinowitz suggests that the word mankind (*bnei adam*) alludes to the Talmudic discussion (Abodah Zarah 2b) about God offering the Torah to each nation and people but none would accept the Torah until He came to the Israelites and they accepted it.

383a. Finkel points out that the original Arabic has "through the master of the prophets" (*i.e.,* Moses) and the discrepancy between the Arabic and the Hebrew version "through the prophets" is probably due to censorship.

384. Literally: His commandment and His warning.

385. Exodus 9:16.

386. Such as the parting of the waters of the Red Sea, the war against Amalek, the miracles at Mt. Sinai and many more.

387. Rabbinowitz cites as examples: *And Israel saw the great work which the Lord did upon the Egyptians . . . and they believed in the Lord and His servant Moses* (Exodus 14:31) and *And the Lord said unto Moses, Lo I come unto thee in a thick cloud, that the people may hear when I speak with thee, and may also believe thee forever* (*ibid.* 19:9).

388. Section 2, Chapter 25.

389. Miracles.

390. Literally: cut off, *i.e.,* premature death as punishment for sin.

391. Resurrection although related to reward and punishment, is not explicitly discussed by God in the Torah because it is not related to this world nor is it a natural phenomenon.

392. Literally: strengthened.

393. Rabbinowitz explains: after many years when the Jews were already in exile in Babylonia.

394. Including Daniel.

395. In his *Guide* (Section 3, Chapter 32), Maimonides also speaks of the gradual development of the whole condition of an individual and the gradual blotting out of all traces of idolatry and the gradual acceptance of the basic tenets of Judaism.

396. Rabbinowitz adds: blessed be He.

397. Exodus 13:17. Rabbinowitz explains: the Israelites who were immersed in slave labor in Egypt for many years had just been liberated and were not yet read to conquer the land of Israel. Therefore, God led them by a circuitous path through the desert to gradually teach them and to train them to wage war.

398. Literally: from them and in them.

399. In physical or worldly matters, *i.e.,* how to wage war.

400. In spiritual matters.

401. Rabbinowitz adds: blessed be He.

402. Rabbinowitz has: very erroneous.

403. By Moses, their leader.

404. Deut. 29:3.

405. See Chapter 26 of Leviticus and Chapter 28 of Deuteronomy. Finkel here cites Maimonides' *Iggeret Teman* where he supports a similar view.

406. The Torah.

407. Rabbinowitz points out that Maimonides believed that the Torah was only given to man to help him perfect his body and soul. Each positive and negative commandment is meant to have man develop an understanding of the true tenets of our faith and to inculcate proper thoughts and ideas in his mind which will lead him to perform good deeds, love and righteousness and hate evil in order to live a full and straight and honorable life. See also the *Guide for the Perplexed* (Section 3, Chapter 32).

408. Rabbinowitz has "matters of (two) worlds" *i.e.,* this world and the world to come. He quotes Deut. 6:24: *And the Lord commanded us to do all these statutes, to fear the Lord our God, for our good always, that He might preserve us alive, as at this day; for our good always* is an allusion to the world to come and *that He might preserve us alive, as at this day* is an allusion to this world.

409. Literally: bitterness.

410. Obeying the word of God allows the Jews to flourish whereas disobedience brings about their downfall.

411. Deut. 28:46.

412. Shabbath 156a.

413. Their happiness and their tribulations.

414. Because this sign proves the miraculous supervision over the Jews by the Lord who rewards or punishes for their good or evil deeds.

415. Rabbinowitz suggests that Maimonides is here referring to the Talmudic story (Shabbath 156b) of the Sage Samuel and the Gentile scholar Ablet who were walking together. Samuel proved to Ablet that Israel's destiny is not under the influence of the constellations but depends upon obedience to the laws of the Torah and that prayer and charity and penitence by Jews can overturn an evil decree of the constellations.

416. Deut. 28:46.

417. Berachoth 5a. This statement clearly indicates that a man's actions determine his fate and destiny.

418. The sun and the moon and the stars and all the constellations of the heaven mentioned in the first part of this Scriptural verse.

419. Deut. 4:19–20.

420. Literally: their matters.

421. Literally: connected to.

422. Literally: the improvement of their matters or their loss.

423. Literally: than the intent of this treatise.

424. Literally: sinking or incorporation into.

425. Literally: the congregation of Korach.

426. Rabbinowitz substitutes: and to certain nations.

427. *I.e.,* the prophet.

428. I Kings 13:3.

429. I Samuel 12:17–18.

430. Levit. Chapter 26 and Deut. Chapter 28.

431. I Samuel 12:17–18.

432. I Kings 13:5.

433. Exodus 10:14.

434. *Ibid.* 9:24.

435. *Ibid.* 9:6.

436. Such as the pestilence which only afflicted the Egyptians.

437. Such as the hail concerning which it is written: *Only in the land of Goshen where the children of Israel were, was there no hail* (Exodus 9:26).

438. Such as the locusts concerning which it is written: *Before them there were no such locusts as they, neither after them shall there be such* (Exodus 10:14).

439. The curses cited in Levit. Chapter 26 and Deut. Chapt. 28 are protracted and recurrent.

440. Levit. 26:21.

441. See also Maimonides' *Guide.* Section 3, Chapter 36.

442. Levit. 26: 27–28.

443. Literally: in matters which are not natural.

444. And never a staff but appeared as such through necromancy.

445. Literally: was completed.

446. Exod. 4:4.

447. See note 424 above.

448. People might consider it a natural phenomenon, *i.e.,* an earthquake.

449. Numbers 16:33.

450. Exodus 14:27.

451. Literally: I flee from.

452. *I.e.,* a miracle.

453. See note 439 above.

454. Rabbinowitz omits the phrase: as we explained.

455. The Israelites.

456. Rabbinowitz explains: instead of showing the Israelites numerous miracles to convince them of the genuineness of the resurrection of the dead, why did God not show them the ultimate miracle; namely, resurrection itself?

457. Literally: messenger.

458. Literally: the decree of wisdom.

459. See Maimonides' *Eight Chapters* (Chapter 8), and his *Hilchoth Yesodei HaTorah* 2: 8–10, and his *Guide for the Perplexed* (Section 1, Chapters 58 and 78 and Section 2, chapter 28).

460. Literally: path.

461. For repeating that which we have already discussed elsewhere, *i.e.*, in the *Commentary on the Mishnah (Chelek* and *Eight Chapters), Mishneh Torah,* and *Guide for the Perplexed.*

462. The explanations of this topic in Maimonides' other writings should have sufficed.

463. Compared to our lengthy remarks in regard to the world to come.

464. Rabbinowitz substitutes: in the book *Guide for the Perplexed,* our composition.

465. *Sifra, Metzorah* s.v. *vechi yithar hazav mizovo.*

466. Proverbs 9:9.

467. Isaiah 28:13.

468. *Ibid.*

469. According to the level of understanding of the reader; for the wise, brevity suffices; for the not so wise, greater length of explanation and commentary may be required.

470. In our oral or written discourses.

471. Rabbinowitz omits the two words "amen" but adds the sentence: treatise completed in the year 1502 of the era used in documents (see section 17 above and note 147).

# The Resurrection Debate

by
Daniel Jeremy Silver

Reprinted with permission from D. J. Silver's *Maimonidean Criticism and the Maimonidean Controversy 1180–1240* (Leiden. E. J. Brill 1965, pp. 109–135).

In 1232 when tension was at its highest, Nachmanides (1194–1270) from Barcelona requested the religious leaders of Castile and Aragon, among others Meir b. Todros Abulafia of Toledo, to join hands in supporting the cause of Solomon b. Abraham of Montpellier. Nachmanides had reason to assume Meir's sympathetic cooperation. Four decades before, this well known Castilian Talmudist had been among the first to challenge Maimonides' works. Nachmanides, however, received more sympathy than cooperation. Meir was battle-scarred and utterly disillusioned. In begging off Meir rationalized his disinvolvement with an *apologia pro sua vita*.[1] Long ago, he had confronted similar communal pressures to those Nachmanides now was experiencing. He had had to go it alone against those who were rebellious against God. He had tried to reach and preach, but to no avail; indeed, not even the wasting of war attendant to an Almohade incursion had traumatized a return. The misguided had failed to see those travails as the corrective punishment of a displeased God.

Meir recalled that even before the *Moreh* had reached Spain, he had recognized the latent danger (latent because it fed the fires of disbelief long since burning in certain quarters) implicit in Maimonides' doctrine of resurrection as formulated in the *Mishneh Torah.* To counter any advantage the enemies of true faith might make of Maimonides' teachings, Meir had written a careful but forthright criticism, a *Sefer Kenaot,* but unfortunately few had shared his concern.

Note the candid admission that his criticism had been motivated more by the social consequences of Maimonides' words than by any intrinsic or substantive position taken in the *Mishneh Torah.*

> I became exercised to protect Israel and its sanctities, to establish the right and its fundaments when I saw that belief in bodily resurrection was being lost in this land among many of its dispersed peoples . . .[2]
>
> Yesteryear and before, even before the book which perplexes the guides (the *Guide for the Perplexed*) had reached here, part of the nation had rebellious ideas about faith in the Creator.[3]

Thirty years before, upon reading the *Mishneh Torah,* Meir had precipitated a flurry of correspondence which he subsequently collated under the title *Kitab al Rasail* (English, *Writings of Controversy*). Knowing this early text and the brouhaha it momentarily touched off, historians have described Meir's attacks as "characterized by great persistence as well as intolerance" and have painted Meir as the archetype of a fanatic pietist, single purposed and single minded in his attitudes.[4]

Scant attention has been paid to an elegy Meir wrote shortly after Maimonides' death in 1204 which must be seen 1) as a plea that an end might be made to the controversy he had started, 2) as evidence of Meir's thorough acquaintance with the *Moreh* and his not unfriendly attitude towards philosophy, and 3) as indication of a not unkindly estimate by Meir of Maimonides the man, and even of the *Moreh.*

> Tears have ceased falling into the [tear] vase for the burning coals within have been kindled.

Why do you ask for yourselves waters from the bottom of my heart when its thoughts have been consumed as with the fires of Hell.

There is just enough [water] for my heart—just enough to extinguish the flames within them. How can they pour [additional] water upon the fires that extinguish my tears.

What happened to the hearts that they despaired of finding a remedy and why has their spirit been broken.

Please ask, if the evil accidents of the times have accosted them and if they groan from the afflictions of the hour.

Or does the raging fire burn because Moses has died—to whom now can they turn (lit., cry out)?

Who will extinguish the fires of sorrow? Who will free the prisoners whose chains have been tightened?

Who will lead us on dry land through seas of knowledge deeper than the depths of the sea?

Who will summon streams of wisdom of the rock? Who will sweeten the bitter waters?

Cease, you who are hungry for instruction — for those about (lit., the people of the day) have broken down her vines.

Weep for the prince of moral instruction who has been taken away. Can you now suckle the poison of asps [as he did]?

He was like a hero in battle. He rejoiced for the day when the chariots of instruction jostled one another in the street.

He was the fruit of life in his group. With his sword he struck through the hearts of his enemies.

He was as the life giving principle and we were as the body. Who of them could live if these would be separated?

Write this upon the walls of the heart and inscribe the wondrous secret on the foreheads of the times.

How the luminaries go down to the grave and how the rocks of instruction were uprooted from their places.

Concerning the much praised one who was buried, it is as if the light left the rocks and preferred to descend to the grave in his place.

Arise, O mighty one, who despised the sweetness of the earth, since today the earth is sweet to his throat (Ed: he has been buried).

Arise, see the people gathered around your grave who kiss its stone and its dust.

Arise, see the scholars of the day — as one — knock on the doors of your understanding as petitioners.

They will ponder your *Mishneh Torah,* daily they will harvest valuable knowledge fashioned as if of pure gold.

They will see in the *Moreh* intellectual steel which flashes as lightning in the darkness.

There they will see the swords of confusion polished clean and honed smooth with the oil of reason.

Words, much desired, as if fashioned like apples of the gold of wisdom in baskets of fit understanding.

Through them the confused came to know truly and through them the weak were strengthened in the fear of their Creator.

Arise [Maimonides], see the sheep who had strayed from secure pens, now following you.

They built with you a sanctuary of instruction; yet today perforce they throw ashes upon their heads (i.e., they mourn).

To whom will they now run for help and, since you are gone, upon whom can they depend?

They will never remove from themselves the yoke of your mourning until the cursed day will remove the yoke of your death (i.e., never).

Alas, the princes tell good news to the counselors of Pharaoh and the seers of that land will smack their lips.

Let not such be heard in the city of Sihon and let not such a piercing groan [be heard] in Heshbon.

It is not a day of good tiding. Be silent lest strangers hear and clap their hands over you.

Would that I might be like a bird, I would fly to his grave. My eyes would summon tears.

I would wet with my tears his dust just as the springs of his knowledge nourished my soul.

I will erode with them (i.e., the tears) the rocks of the time (i.e., the mighty) just as the waters of his suffering wear down great men.

What else can the cursed days say? What more can they complain about? How can they justify themselves?

Is there still any answer in their mouthing to the complaints? Will they fault us that they may be justified?

Are the sins of the waters of Meribah (i.e., of controversy) still remembered today? Do they still pursue us?

Or is the hand of evil days waxing strong — days that spread hurt in their anger.

Tearing prey until its lair is filled with corpses. One crowds out another in his grave.

Children will be buried in the very grave of their fathers; for if not how will there be sufficient space for his victims.

This is the ancient law (i.e., destruction). These have learnt from them — he consecrated these disciples.

Where are the dead of yesteryear? Only a short time has passed. Where have they disappeared?

Did the host of night kidnap them? Were they not exiled from the populous city? How did we not cry?

Rather they [these days] despised us — therefore they forced us from pleasant dwellings unto parched wilderness.

If on a day their children are vexed they are not troubled: if they [the children] become weak it is passed off.

If they will call them no one answers. When they speak bitterly it is as the braying of an ass.

Will you call in their ears when no one listens? Will you groan or be silent?

Today they groan for their wandering . . .[5]

You are like them (the former evil times) except that they hastened
and you are slow to pass over.

Search out the world, ask even of the gates of Hell — for there her
great ones are shackled.

See the grave of Moses. It is a sign to all created beings that death is
unavoidable.

He (Maimonides) has disappeared but not his greatness. Though he
is gone his deeds are here.

Peace to you, O faithful messenger, peace. As with the groaning
over the slain they groan for you.

Peace, you whose righteousness was like a river, the living feel bitterly deprived by your death.

Peace, they cling to you today with a love like my love or the love of
the angels of righteousness.

In measure as your soul desired righteousness, so the angels of
righteousness desired you.

May peace hover over you just as justice and peace were joined
always in you.[6]

Meir can not be figured as unreservedly anti-philosophic. He
had disapproved of certain arguments, but not of the whole. One
senses that youthful brashness had carried him farther than he had
wished, and that he now sensed that it was not Maimonides he had
been arguing against, but a widespread contagion of religious
indifference and skepticism for which the lion of the Law, the
pious Maimonides could hardly be blamed. In any case external
threat, "cursed days," required that those who would wield the rod
of correction now moderate their efforts.[7]

Israel stumbled into a Maimonidean controversy. It was not
fear of philosophy nor ignorance of philosophy which precipitated
it but a breakdown of faith among certain elements within the
western communities, among anonymous persons who when
pressed claimed the *Moreh* and the *Mada* as support of their fan-

cies.[8] Doubters and sophisticates seized on certain quotations — often out of context — in Maimonides or from philosophic material generally and arrogated these as proof texts of their denials. To blame the *Moreh Zedek,* Maimonides, for this sputtering of the candle of disbelief was on the face of it implausible. Nor was philosophy to blame. There is no indication that individual anti-Maimonids studied the *Moreh,* or Bahya, or Saadya, or ha-Levi any less assiduously or appreciatively than the Maimonids. Judah Alfakhar, to cite a classic anti-Maimonid example, was knowledgeable and competent in philosophic disciplines.[9]

In this first stage of the controversy, before the *Moreh* was known, the less than pious believed that they found some support in the *Mishneh Torah* for their denial of the traditional assumption of resurrection. To defend against this challenge, those who vigorously opposed such aberrations perforce attacked the delineation Maimonides had given to this doctrine.

Resurrection had been affirmed rather than defined by the rabbinic tradition. Typically, the early 13th century scholar Zerahyah ha-Yevani:

> It is well known that one ought to believe that when man dies full of good deeds and having lived a pious life God will love him and in the nature of this love is the reward beggaring description. . . . We ought not to search out how this reward actually will take place.[10]

When Maimonides in his *Commentary to the Mishnah, Sanhedrin X* argued man's inability "to comprehend the delight of the soul" in the future life on the basis that such delights were outside the limits of sense experience and hence beyond the capacity of human reason, he was simply handling methodically doctrinal reservations many had long observed. Touching the doctrine of physical resurrection many had observed poetic license as long as the tenet itself was supported.

In brief, rabbinic doctrine insisted on some future reward but was open-ended on the specifics of that reward. The 15th century philosopher Joseph Albo explained this deliberately uncertain certainty.

> But it [Resurrection] is not itself either a fundamental or a derivative principle of divine law in general or of the Law of Moses in particular, for they can be conceived without it. As long as one believes in reward and punishment generally, whether corporeal, in this world, or spiritual, in the world to come, he does not deny a principle of the Law of Moses if he disbelieves in resurrection. Nevertheless it is a dogma accepted by our nation, and everyone professing the Law of Moses is obliged to believe it . . . Belief in the Messiah and in the resurrection of the dead are principles peculiar to Christianity which cannot be conceived without them. But resurrection and the Messiah [in Judaism] are like branches issuing from the principles of Reward and Punishment and are not root principles in themselves.[11]

Resurrection was the most "unenlightened" rabbinic dogma; that is, it was the religious dogma which most violated the *tendenz* of Greek philosophy which throughout assumed the dualism of body and soul. An ancient veneration and a long lingering issue, it had been hotly debated as early as the first century.[12] Circumscribed by the authority of traditional belief but convinced of the accuracy of Platonic psychology, medieval thinkers resorted to equivocation. Resurrection seemed to these a crude, even superstitious doctrine — quite out of step with any proper understanding of the soul and its faculties and the body and its foibles. If both pious and philosophic, these men could cite precedent for their seeming heterodoxy. The traditional treatment of resurrection was anything but consistent. Raba had insisted that Job 7:9 ("As the cloud is consumed and vanisheth away, so he that goeth down to the pit shall come up no more") indicated a Biblical denial of the entire doctrine.[13] Ecclesiastes presented a skeptical view of the whole issue, as did *Ben Sira*.[14] If the liturgy praised a God "who raises the dead," Biblical literature raised no such definite promise.[15]

Resurrection did not remain the controversial theme for many reasons: 1) Maimonides affirmed even as he squirmed. Men recalled that Maimonides had established in his introductory commentary to Mishnah *Sanhedrin* the belief in physical resurrection as a cardinal tenet of the faith and few had the interest or the patience to square subsequent discursive elaboration with this simple declaration. 2) With the Hebrew translation of the *Moreh* a veritable Pandora's box of theologic topics was provided. 3) Physical resurrection was the weak point of rabbinic apologetics. Even the most traditional disciples often had quite esoteric views and whatever their public professions entertained personal reservations. One does not attack another for struggling with one's private doubts.

Meir, however, was horror-stricken at Maimonides' seeming denial of bodily resurrection in the *Mishneh Torah*.[16] This promise was part of God's covenant with Israel.[17] He could not support Maimonides in deducing that there will be neither form nor body in the *Olam ha-Ba* from the single text "that in the *Olam ha-Ba* there is neither eating nor drinking."[18] The reprise in Meir's apoplexy was his argument that Maimonides' view destroyed the substance of God's promise, so essential to faith. "If bodies will not be resurrected how can the promise of a redeemed Israel be fulfilled."[19] "If God does not resurrect where is the hope for those who at great personal sacrifice obey His law."[20] As for the metaphysical problem involved, is such an act too much for God?

Reduced to simple terms — and Meir's first missive has the virtue of simplicity and is, therefore, revealing — Meir argued that faith is not a selfless commitment. Israel's faith is based on a covenant, a two-way relationship, man obeys and God abides. The obligations of this covenant for the party of the second part (God) require the arrival of the Messiah and a proper occasion for the resurrection of the faithful. One can sympathize, for without hope the spirit shrivels, and what hope had Israel, what justification for continuing its intransigent confrontation of Diaspora and despair, except this promise?

Meir's outpouring was submitted to Jonathan ha-Kohen, for

what specific purpose it is hard to tell. Jonathan was a respected senior, a man of known *halachic* competence, piety, and prestige. Perhaps Jonathan's correspondence with Maimonides and his sponsorship of the translation of the *Moreh* made him the logical addressee. Meir certainly felt that Lunel had shown an exaggerated admiration for their intellectual mentor, but he made no request explicit or implicit that the work be banned.[21]

Meir appended to the resurrection missive a longish set of *halachic* glosses to the *Mishneh Torah*. Perhaps he hoped by this display of erudition to establish his credentials. Their provenance is difficult to assess. Six of the points touched were to issues raised by Jonathan in his correspondence with Maimonides;[22] three of the others touched points raised by Rabad[23] (Moses ha-Kohen had notes also on these); one was entirely original — the first,[24] as were elements of the notes to *M. T. Abodah Zarah* 2:7 and 4:2. Meir's method throughout was juridic. The points at issue were largely theoretical: whether a month may be intercalated during a Sabbatical year or a year of famine under certain extenuating circumstances (in Meir's day the calendar was already fixed); whether children are to suffer the death penalty if they live in a condemned apostate city (such a city could exist only in an independent Israel); whether an elder who renders a verdict in spirit contrary to a decision of the Sanhedrin is liable to the death penalty if the matter involved a violation not specifically described by a Biblical negative commandment, i.e., in ritual matters of Phylacteries, Lulav, Sabbath (there was, of course, no longer a Sanhedrin). The only issues having contempoary relevance were cited from the circulating Jonathan-Maimonides correspondence: whether a mezuzah required a specifically prepared parchment; whether one may carry a found object on the Sabbath, etc.

Meir's approach was not heavily negative. He conceded the *Mishneh Torah's* worth.[25] Interestingly, he made no challenge to Maimonides' code method except such as was implicit by the opening up of seemingly settled issues. He contented himself with suggesting that "there is no wheat without chaff" and that this represents but a small anthology of the "leaves which he [Meir] had plucked."[26]

Meir's answer, for some unrecoverable reason, came not from Jonathan ha-Kohen but from Aaron b. Meshullam (d. 1210), son of the venerable founder patron of the Lunel school. In tone Aaron's epistle was a "dressing down," as if Meir had been called on the carpet by a college dean. "Know, my brother, that humility is the adornment of wisdom and its sweetness, while arrogance is her flux and disease."[27] "Your legal issues having nothing new in them and reading between the lines of your letter it is apparent that you did not want to set a matter straight in your own thought but to preen your intellect."[28] Meir was accused of rashness, arrogance, brashness, ignorance, and subjected to condescension. "I know you did not consult your wise and venerable father."[29] To Aaron, Meir was the prodigal who brashly challenged the experience, understanding, and knowledge of a master without having mastered even fundamentals. "Take to heart, my son, the rabbinic admonition 'that one who argues with his teacher is as one who argues with the *Shekinah.'*"[30]

Presumptuousness was Meir's cardinal sin. He ought to have inquired, not pontificated.[31] He has asked Lunel how they could praise Maimonides. "Know that such praise does not begin to exhaust Maimonides' accomplishments."[32] His teachings are "clean, healthy, and worthy."[33] His knowledge is catholic of all sources and traditions.[34] Indeed, God sent Moses to the people at an opportune time when "the hand of the judges had grown lax" and the control of Israel had become progressively more difficult.[35] In this time of confusion Maimonides "stretched out the staff of his strength over the sea of the Talmud until it was possible for his children to enter the sea in safety."[36] "Behold it is written before me and I will not deny it that from the days of Rabbina and R. Ashi none arose in Israel equal to Maimonides to multiply counsel and increase redemption."[37] Not only is Maimonides' genius and knowledge unparalleled but there is none in Israel whose family tree is so redolent of rabbis and learned ancestors.[38]

Aaron's defense of Maimonides' views on resurrection was made simply. How can Meir have been so naive as to presume that the single statement of *M. T. Teshubah* 8:2 exhausted Maimonides' treatment of the subject. Had Meir noticed the many places in the *Mishneh Torah* where anyone who denied the belief in resurrection was labeled a *Kofer* or an *Epicoros* or *Min*?[39] "Now we will set you straight as to that which you said concerning the servant of God that he denies the Covenant and destroys the hope of those who dwell in this life."[40]

Basic to Aaron's view was the argument that one ought not accept the exoteric meaning of the *aggada*. Aaron transformed Maimonides into a disciple of Saadya who got around conflicting *aggadic* texts by positing two resurrections, one during the Messianic Age followed by a second death and a second period of resurrection in the *Olam ha-Ba*, a totally new world where the properties of space and time and bodies — all the worldly categories — no longer apply.[41] Maimonides' statement denying bodily attributes referred only to the *Olam ha-Ba*. Meir was accused of not being conversant with such Saadyanic subtleties,[42] indeed, "you ought not to have approached this whole area steeped in mystery until you had spent much time exploring the whole matter with some learned master, for in your epistle you show that you do not have the faintest acquaintance with such mysteries."[43]

This attempt to impose a Saadyanic superstructure on Maimonides is interesting a) in showing that only a limited knowledge of Maimonides' views was then available to his protagonists (the *Ma'amar Tehiyyat ha-Metim* was not translated by Judah al Harizi until 1198 and the text of Part III of the *Moreh* did not reach the Languedoc until 1200), b) as illustrating the quick proliferation of ideas through translation. Judah ibn Tibbon had completed his Hebrew translation, the first, of the *Emunot ve De'ot* as late as 1186. It obviously had helped to organize many loosely held verbal traditions popular in the Jewish schools.

Aaron returned two letters. The second was a point by point rebuttal of Meir's *halachic* glosses in which Aaron set each point out fully in all its tradition, logic, judgment, ramification, etc.[44]

Aaron extended himself most on the challenge raised to *M. T. Issure Bi'ah* 15:3 where Maimonides had ruled that an Israelite who had relations with a *mamzer* (a child of an illegally constituted marriage) without a proper marriage was not to be stripped since the Talmud prescribed such punishment (in the area of illicit marriages) only in the single case of a High Priest who married a widow or divorcee. Maimonides here had ruled against a traditional consensus. Indeed, he had admitted to Jonathan that he once had thought otherwise.[45] Any ruling depended on the interpretation of an involved Talmudic debate.[46] The uniformity of dissent by Rabad, Moses ha-Kohen, the sages of Lunel, and Meir underscored its novelty and Aaron was forced to some lengths to establish Maimonides' view. His method here, as in all his responsa, was to review the Talmud discussions and to show how Maimonides' opinion was plausible.

Aaron argued not the absolute correctness of Maimonides' decisions, but their plausibility.[47] "This is the opinion of Maimonides as I understand it, but if you wish to have another opinion, go ahead — the Torah has seventy faces; what is unacceptable is your presumption of Maimonides' light-handed treatment of the material and your claim that he was unaware of conflicting traditions."[48] This last paragraph is crucial for any understanding of the *Mishneh Torah*'s reception in the west. In the east, in Yemen for instance, it became a constitution — *the* law — while among even its greatest admirers in France and Spain it remained but another, albeit brilliant, contribution to *halachic* literature. Not one of the better scholar defenders swore unquestioning fealty. Nor can any glossater *ipso facto* be presumed to have disparaged the entire work.

Meir did not let matters ride. "Oh staff of Aaron, is not your nature to freshen the waters — why do you now roil them?"[49] Meir took understandable umbrage at Aaron's high-handed questioning of his competence. "Keep your own view and I'll keep mine."[50] His anger extended to a petty grammatical criticism of certain forms and meters Aaron had employed in his opening poetry.[51] Meir had turned to Lunel knowing their scholarly reputation and believing they accepted "the rule among the wise in such matters that when a proper argument is developed all acknowledge it."[52] Apparently this was not to be. "Now you listen . . . and if you are really open minded, I know that you will find that I am right."[53]

For Meir the proofs of resurrection were clear. They appeared in the Torah (Gen. 13:16, 26:3, 28:13; Deut. 1:8, 11:9, 11:21, 32:27), in the Prophets (I Sam. 2:6, Isa. 26:11, 42:11; Ezek. 27:10; Hos. 6:2), in the Writings (Ps. 72:16, 104:30, 50:4–5; Dan. 12:2, 12:13; Job 7:9; Eccl. 9:4–6), in the Talmud (*T. B. Sanhedrin* 90b–91a; *T. B. Berachot* 17a, etc.). Especially clear to Meir were the texts dealing with bodily reward and punishment in the *Olam ha-Ba* (*M. Abot* 4:5: *T. B. Sanhedrin* 90b–92a; *T. B. Sanhedrin* 90b–92a, 99a; *T. B. Abodah Zarah* 26a, etc.).

These texts were not to be handled casually or interpreted cavalierly. True, they contained allegorical depths but in no case was their establishment of bodily resurrection in the *Olam ha-Ba* to be reasoned away.[54] Meir quoted Saadya to his own purpose; had not the Gaon held that in only four types of Biblical texts could there be any question of a wholly metaphorical intent — none of these cases being applicable here.[55]

Meir showed insight into the burden of Aaron's position. His was an attempt to establish the philosophically popular concept of the immortality of the soul, while retaining the traditional emphasis on resurrection largely because being hoary it could not be discarded.[56] *T. B. Berachot* 17a must be the controlling text. In this text where R. Gamaliel had stated that there is no eating and drinking in the world to come he establishes not the concept of the immortality of the soul but that of physical resurrection;[57] for why should he preclude the existence of specific bodily attributes if there was no possibility that bodies might exist in the *Olam ha-Ba* to which one might be tempted to make such an attribution.[58]

Meir could not imagine how reward and punishment can operate in the *Olam ha-Ba* if bodies were not there to receive their due "according to their corruption or quality"[59] "for have not our sages said that the souls do not receive their reward or punishment in the *Olam ha-Ba* except conjoined to their bodies."[60]

The argument had shifted imperceptibly but inevitably to an issue which would be aired throughout the 13th century — the permissible limits of the allegorical interpretation of Scripture. We shall hear of some philosophers who denied the reality of all Biblical stories, considering them to be mere allusions to philosophic doctrines. Some Kabbalists will come close to this view and will insist that had the Bible simply told the stories of Esau and Hagar, Laban and Jacob, Balaam's ass, and the like, and not impregnated these stories with esoteric meaning, far greater books could have been written.[61] Meir possessed an acute sense of religious preservation and sought to limit such exegesis. Otherwise, he averred, the law must follow the narrative out the window and the entire foundation of the commandments which establish Jewish life would be undermined.[62]

Meir's architecture of the future bliss is clear. There are some who are wholly righteous who will live on from this life to the Messianic Age.[63] In the Messianic Age many of the saintly of Israel will be resurrected[64] and they will live on until the more inclusive resurrection scheduled for the *Olam ha-Ba* takes place. "The Talmud is full on every side of clear proof concerning the *Olam ha-Ba* that it is the end of the rewards for the righteous and of the punishments of the wicked and involves both body and substance. God forbid, that any who fear God should deny this."[65]

Meir wrote his first and second letters to Lunel some time before Maimonides' death. As might be anticipated, he was not satisfied with Aaron's reply and either in 1204 or shortly before he addressed himself to certain rabbis of Sarfat, seven by name: Solomon of Meroz, Isaac b. Abraham of Dampierre, Simson b. Abraham of Sens, Simson of Corbeil, David of Chateaux Thierry, Abraham of Toul, and Eliezer b. Aaron of Bourgogne. Meir asked these worthies to judge the merits of his correspondence and to submit to Aaron a position paper on resurrection and on the other Talmudic issues which he had raised.

All you who dwell on earth, all you who inhabit the land, You men, our kinsmen, who are sturdy of faith; be zealous for the Rod (God)

who created in His might all creation which swarms over the land
and the seas.

Judge! Take no account of rank! Let rich and poor come as one to
justice.

That those who permit judgment may see and know clearly that
there are in the land judges who judge honestly.[66]


In this letter Meir touched rhetorically his motivation in
entering the fray and answered quite simply that he wished all doctrine to be carefully regulated. Meir was concerned with the
promise of the faith. If resurrection is but a mirage which dissi-
pates itself upon scrutiny, what is the hope for "all the oppressed
lost in the lands of their captivity."[67] The certainty which encour-
ages Israel is the belief in "a day when God will repay all according
to his righteousness or innocence." How can wound be repaid for
wound and sorrow for sorrow, if God does not cause all creatures
to be reestablished in form and body?"[68] "What profit is there that
men should obey His commandments and go about sadly because
of the Lord God. If bodies are not resurrected where then is their
hope and who will regulate this hope?"[69]

A historian must add that religionists become concerned with
the promise of faith when this promise is not self evident. Meir's
energy reflected a dissipation of that loyalty and a fear of the social
consequences of this loss of confidence.

To his now familiar arguments Meir appended his equally
familiar glosses in a clear, precise form obviously reworked for the
occasion.[70]

Of or for the French rabbis Simson b. Abraham of Sens (c.
1155 — 1225) replied. His letter is to be dated shortly after Maimonides' death.[71]

Simson was and remained a Talmudist working in a Talmudically oriented community. The issue of resurrection did not excite
him. The whole issue was, after all, cut and dried. The famous text
*T. B. Berachot* 17a indicated only that there would be no eating or
drinking or sex in a worldly sense. The resurrected will draw their
nourishment and drink from the divine radiance. As proof he

offered *T. B. Sanhedrin* 90a, 92b, 108a.[72] Body and soul will be resurrected together as they will be saved and judged together.[73] The holoistic rabbinic view of man is confidently reasserted. Simson's understanding of the textual problems insisted that what difficulties arise occur because interpreters did not differentiate the Messianic Age from the *Olam ha-Ba* (not unlike Maimonides' own reconciliation in his *Ma'amar Tehiyyat ha-Metim*). There are truly righteous who do not die.[74] Some souls are given to bodies eternally. For others there is death and rebirth in the *Olam ha-Ba*. The Messianic Age is a period of resurrection for a favored few, but principally the time when God releases Israel from captivity. The *Olam ha-Ba* is a newly created world without the properties of this worldly existence. But unlike Maimonides' view, the body's identity is not wholly lost. God grafts the wings of an eagle to these resurrected bodies and they hover, not unlike the angelic beings, over the face of the deep.[75]

In a second letter to Meir, Simson confronted the problem of allegoric interpretation. He quoted *T. B. Hullin* 90b, that in only three cases was the *aggada* to be taken in other than its literal meaning. Of philosophic flights of fancy based on the *aggada,* a mistake for which he fingered Aaron, Simson also had serious reservations. Such sophistries are not unlike "passing the proverbial elephant through the eye of a needle."[76] Presumably in all other cases an exoteric interpretation was required. In a postscript to this second letter he quoted in further confirmation Saadya's four categories of permissible allegorical interpretation. The *Emunot ve De'ot* had just arrived in Sens and had been read out to him by one who possessed the necessary linguistic skills.

*Halacha* concerned Simson primarily. It is doubtful that he knew or sensed the social ramifications of the resurrection debate. Abraham b. Nathan of Lunel, who was with Simson at this time and subsequently traveled to Castile, chronicled on his arrival in Toledo that only now (in Toledo) had he met any who said that Maimonides had denied resurrection and had taught only the doctrine of the immortality of the soul.[77] In France such comment as had been expressed had been entirely *halachic.*

As *halachist* Simson dealt not only with Meir's questions, but with Lunel's twenty-four, and showed his thorough acquaintance with the *Mishneh Torah* and Maimonides' correspondence. He first discussed the six questions revived by Meir which had been covered also in the Jonathan-Maimonides correspondence.[78] He handled these in the familiar form of legal debate, citation, source, argument. His purpose "is not to establish law but to let the erudite hear and then let anyone who wishes to answer him do so."[79] Even when he agreed with Maimonides' ruling, as in the case of the special requirements for parchment in a mezuzah scroll, Simson was eager to make clear certain sophisticated differences in their reasoning.[80]

Simson acknowledged the extraordinary needs of the time which had prompted Maimonides to write the *Mishneh Torah,* but faulted him severely for his lack of citations. This is not the way of *halacha.* Let those who want to know study the original texts which permit various lines of reasoning and development.[81] Finally in a second letter he added an extensive gloss of his own to *M. T. Parah Adumah* 11:2 in which he challenged Maimonides' view that one who has been contaminated by corpse uncleanness and has undertaken the first cleansing may, if a delay is unavoidable, undergo the second required sprinkling at any time. The argument was based on a correlation of two variant texts, *T. B. Haggigah* 22b and *T. B. Kiddushin* 62a.

Simson's further role as a Maimonidean critic is uncertain. He wrote one more brief response to a second letter from Meir, pleading with Meir that he had no time to prolong such a point by point *halachic* correspondence.[82] Meir's questions were purposeless — matters ought not to be raised unless they have been brought into serious question. Enough had been said.

Simson throughout respected Maimonides as *halachist* although he questioned his methods. It is, therefore, difficult to know what to make of Abraham Maimonides' report that later in Simson's life he became active in opposing Maimonides. The facts are these. Simson was among some three hundred French and English sages who pilgrimaged to the Holy Land circa 1211 or 1212, probably motivated by messianic expectation. Abraham

Maimonides, in his *Milhamot Adonai,* reported and made much of the fact that Simson did not stop in Alexandria to pay his respects; the implication is that the oversight was deliberate, and that once settled in Acre and still later in Jerusalem Simson continued to argue against various teachings of his father. Saracheck[83] among others makes much of this, but Abraham's own words make us feel that the issues raised were purely *halachic.*

> And, I heard concerning R. Simson the master of Tosaphot who was in Acre, whom we did not meet because he did not pass by here — we heard about him after his death and about one of his pupils that they disputed the teaching of my Father and Teacher in some few matters. The particular issues were not set right by us because we did not examine them. We said to ourselves, if these words contain truth let them eat the fruit of their labor and if not they will be publicly denied.[84]

The only reason to believe that "resurrection" continued to be an issue is the succeeding sentence in Abraham Maimonides' text which mentions without specification certain men who propagated "the profession of a faith false in basic principle" in the various communities of the Near East. The precise relation, if any, of this charge to Simson is uncertain. To all this only two other historical rumors can be added: according to Abraham Zacuto (15 c.), a R. Caleb, a disciple of Maimonides, otherwise unknown, disputed these issues with Simson,[85] and a rumor reported by Abraham Maimonides himself which averred that he had excommunicated Simson — a rumor which he flatly denied.[86]

Simson leads us to the interesting figure of the wandering Provençal scholar Abraham b. Nathan ha-Yarhi (c. 1155–1215), one of the leading anthologists of the variant religious customs of the day. The only published version of *Kitab al Rasail* includes a cryptic heading after Meir's first letter to Simson, "Afterward there came from France a response to my letter from R. Abraham b. Nathan of Lunel and this is its text"[87] — but no text follows. Higger overlooked this heading, but he succeeded in establishing on other grounds that a known commentary to *Kallah Rabbati* was the work of this Abraham and he has published that portion of the commentary which dealt with the exchange of letters between Simson and Meir and is in point of fact a continuation of the resurrection debate.[88] We know from other sources that this Provençal scholar studied with the Tosaphist Isaac b. Samuel before he settled in Toledo, Meir's home, in 1204. He was bilingual (Arabic-Hebrew),[89] and it is not impossible that it was he who translated the Saadya passages in Simson's hearing.

Professing great admiration for Maimonides, whom he called Gaon, Abraham quoted the sources in the *Mishneh Torah* where Maimonides had stated that those who deny resurrection have no place in the world to come. Like Simson, Abraham could not see why Meir had raised all this fuss. Maimonides' theories may have been in error, but he cannot be faulted for any denial of the fundament of resurrection. But certainly Meir had thought so and Abraham paraphrased Meir's arguments, cited Aaron's high-handed reply, and quoted Simson at length.[90] He omitted all reference to the accompanying *halachic* debate. Abraham concluded by adducing other proof of Simson's views.

Abraham was troubled by a seeming contradiction between Ps. 72:16 and *T. B. Berachot* 17a. The Psalm speaks of redemption in glowing terms, concluding "may he be as a rich cornfield in the land upon the tops of the mountains," which Abraham understood as an allusion to certain future gastronomic rewards. How then establish both this promise and the oft cited "There is no eating or drinking . . ."? Obviously, the one refers to eating in the Messianic Age and the other to non-eating in the *Olam ha-Ba.* "Bodily resurrection is not an attribute of the Messianic Age."[91] The Messianic Age will mark the end of Israel's captivity and dispersion. The *Olam ha-Ba* will mark the salvation of the righteous. Some may live on into the Messianic Age, but resurrection *per se* is of the *Olam ha-Ba,* where "God will give life to the body and soul together . . . and judge them according to the measure of justice."[92] Abraham's views and Simson's were, then, essentially one — as was their attitude toward Meir's tempest in a teapot.[93]

Crucial to an understanding of the world view of those who at this stage enthusiastically supported the Maimonidean position is the activity of the wealthy physician-literati-sometime scholar Sheshet ha-Nasi b. Isaac of Saragossa (1131–1210), also known as Sheshet b. Isaac Benveniste.[94] Sheshet was *Alfaquim* (physician) and bailiff to Alfonso II and Pedro II of Aragon and possibly the wealthiest and most powerful Jew of his time. That a Jew of this rank became enmeshed in the *Kitab al Rasail* debate offers effective testimony to its notoriety. Sheshet ha-Nasi b. Isaac of Saragossa entered the fray with a letter sent to Lunel in rebuttal to the first polemic addressed by Meir to Jonathan and before Meir had received Aaron's original answer. In this letter Sheshet dismissed out of hand the *halachic* arguments of the Meir-Aaron correspondence. He probably lacked the necessary tools for legal debate. Only one *halachic* issue was even alluded to — the question of the mezuzah, and then only to give an opportunity for Sheshet to inveigh *ad hominem* against a writer who, despite his inconsequence, showed such unbecoming disrespect for excellence. Meir was ticked off as a presumptuous pup.[95] Sheshet was but little interested in the involvements of rabbinic tradition. His letter does include a few remarks of a Midrashic nature,[96] but it is clear that Sheshet thought in and depended upon a philosophic rather than a Talmudic frame of reference. It is the philosophic plausibility of resurrection which alone concerned him.[97]

Sheshet began by arguing the immutability of natural law.[98] Biblically, "there is nothing new under the sun" (Eccl. 1:9). Philosophically, God at creation gave to each created thing its natural form and these, consequently, obey God by abiding their essential nature.[99] Bodies, by definition, have appetites. To argue that God resurrects bodies without appetites is a contradiction in terms.[100]

What of the argument that the Creator of all, being omnipotent, can change at will the nature of His order and resurrect in bodily form without appetite? God could — but He has not. "We ought not say God can until we see that He has."[101] Furthermore, a change in the basic order of things would imply an imperfection in the original creation and in the Creator.

Does Sheshet deny all possibility of miracles? Here Sheshet's hardiness deserted him. He equivocated. He argued that God had interfered in the natural order but only occasionally to help out His people and His prophets.[102] For all practical purposes God has never touched the basic framework of the world.

> To change the seasons, to refashion the circuit of the planets, or to remake the nature of fire so that smoke would descend rather than rise or to reverse the order of water so that it would rise instead of settling or in the case of any other created thing which exists changeless by virtue of God's will — of such things we have no knowledge nor have our ancestors reported any occasions since Day One when God injected into such things a wholly new nature which became established permanently (rather than temporarily). So Solomon: "That which has been is that which shall be and that which has been done is that which shall be done and there is nothing new under the sun." (Eccl. 1:9).[103]

To Sheshet resurrection presupposed such a basic change in the natural order.[104] What then is resurrection? "The pleasure of the intellect which cleaves to its Creator."[105] The philosophic immortality of the activated intellect freed of its prison body,[106] freed of all mortal attributes, and rejoicing in the effulgence of God.[107] Resurrection will not take place at any one time in the future but occurs daily.[108] It does not rupture the material order of things, but is the happy result of that potential which God placed within certain men at their birth.[109] The intellect, once activated, can live forever. If sages or tradition spoke otherwise, i.e., of an actual return of soul to body, it was only to "reassure the simple" who could not accept a more refined promise,[110] and, incidentally, could not achieve such salvation. Why does the Bible seem to allude to Heaven and physical resurrection? The Bible speaks allegorically[111] to strengthen the faith of the simple, to encourage by the promise of reward and to frighten into obedience by the threat of punishment.[112]

Comparing Meir's approach to Sheshet's, we note the widely

disparate authority in which each grounded his case. Sheshet argued from sense experience, Meir from Scripture. Meir quoted the Talmud. His problem was exegetic — what did a text really mean. Sheshet brushed off these interpretive problems. His authorities were Epicurus, Plato, and Aristotle.[113] His problem was to interpret science accurately. Sheshet set little store with those who claimed unique authority for revelation. Man's innate reason had enabled many not aware of the truths of Sinaitic revelation to acknowledge God's unity.[114] Revelation had established the truths of theology, but Sheshet believed that these truths were not recondite but accessible to human reason. Meir was concerned with the possible undermining of Scriptural authority by the practice of unbridled allegorical interpretation. Sheshet blithely stated, "All the words of the prophets are meant as allegories and have hidden meanings."[115] Sheshet's epistle was not so much a defense of Maimonides or of the *Mishneh Torah* (both praised but never cited) as a defense of the first principles of philosophic speculation. Sheshet remained as indifferent to the various resurrection formulas of *M. T. Teshubah* as he did to Meir's Midrashic exegesis. What Sheshet praised in Maimonides was not his *halachic* competence nor even his philosophy, but his interest in philosophy. Maimonides was "the man of God, the holy one, the Gaon, the philosopher who excelled all others, possessed of a full knowledge of his creator who served God with his mind and understanding."[116] Immediately he continued: "Thus did the ancient wise men say that one can serve his Creator only if he knows His true nature and only if God has permitted His spirit to him or if he be a philosopher who by virtue of his ability approaches God."[117] At issue between Meir and Sheshet was the basis of faith. Was faith a preserve of the brilliant, its truths accessible to reason, its salvation limited to the mentally alert and philosophically disciplined, or was it "the inheritance of all Israel," its truths accessible in Scripture, its salvation universal and not limited to the erudite?

One reviews Sheshet's passion for philosophic norms in two acerbic poems he indited against Meir.

I will break, I will prick, the words of Meir and I will not leave any remnant to him.

He closed the doors of understanding with his two hands, Lying lips are his portion.

He contemns knowledge, he gathered his strength from the riffraff.

The lightness of his head spoiled his judgment. He increased his lies, He enlarged his sin.

He discharged his arrows against the *Moreh*; He is the son of a rebellious son; Have no regard for him.

He enlarged with evil intent, like the son of Edom. He nests his trust on gossamer.

Even against his master he became arrogant. He gnashed his teeth because of his great folly.

If God is a form, and he believes according to the literal meaning, he denied his God.

For if God is corporeal, having a hand or eye, any form, God would be mortal and have no permanent existence.

Therefore, he lied for he did not march out between the light of dawn and the pitch darkness of night.

His song is an anthology of nothing. As a magician he gets involved in a quarrel which is not his.[118]

And again:

My friends asked me, how can one be named Meir (i.e., one who gives light) when he is one who walks in darkness.

I answered them: The sages have already called the night, light. His name is among those similarly transposed.[119]

Again, besides any private bad blood between these two of which we are historically unaware, what is at issue is not the *Mishneh Torah* nor even resurrection, but Sheshet's passion for a God who is not only nonanthropomorphic but pure being. Sheshet dismissed Meir's theology as systematically crude and simplistic:

If God is form, and he believes according to the literal meaning, he denies God.

For if God is corporeal, having a head or eyes, any form, God would be mortal and have no permanent existence.

This attack is passing strange, in that a) in the *Kitab al Rasail* Meir does not define his God concept, and b) Meir's own religious poetry breathes the pure air of monotheism unadulterated by any of the fanciful speculations associated with the *Shiur Komah* or the *Alef Bet de R. Akiba*. Compare these lines selected from one of Meir's hymns lauding God's power.

How will you ascribe form to that which has no body? How can He be like the bodies? Who can circumscribe and gather in His essence?

He is the beginning without end, How can there be end or boundary to the Creator and Fashioner of all?

He is strong and the source of strength and power, He is merciful and the source of His mercy and righteousness.

He lives, From him alone is the fountain of life for all living things, He is beyond the source of His holiness.

He exists but without place. How can place circumscribe Him, He created its [earth's] dust and dimension?

He was before the dimension of time, how can time relate to Him since He created its seconds and minutes? . . .[120]

Wherein lay the parting of the ways?

Men like Sheshet began with the necessity of a pristine and philosophically acceptable God concept: that is, one free of all attributes and relations. Men like Meir presumed God's oneness and otherness and began with the necessity of a God who could reveal and resurrect. Both insisted on *Yihud*, God's oneness. Each believed he insisted on God's otherness. But by *Yihud* men like Meir meant God's uniqueness and spirituality and men like Sheshet God's uniqueness and the logic of God's pure existence. *Yihud* to the Talmudically oriented rabbis meant a God of whom one ought not posit human attributes, yet a God who had the power of creation and of judgment and of resurrection. *Yihud* to the speculative meant the *ding an sich* — the unmoved mover — of whom it could only be said that He is. The world was created by God but ran according to natural law. Such a view allowed precious little leeway for such fundamentals of faith as prayer, revelation, and resurrection. To argue as Meir had argued the possibility of divine interference with natural law was to the speculative *prima facie* evidence of an imperfect God idea. Presumably such a belief could be sustained only by assuming positive attributes of God.

One can describe the prevailing rationalism as a backwash of the high tide of the Arabian cultural sea, but how account for those who held to it? One suspects that at base it was a matter of education and environment. Those educated in the *yeshibot* clung to the sanctities or transmuted their speculative energies into mystical and conforming channels. Those privately tutored were grounded in the Biblical aspects of faith but not its *halachic* reaches and probably knew as much of Greek science and logic as they did of Talmud — if not more. Furthermore, these men generally moved in the cosmopolitan circles of early 13th century Spain and Provence and rubbed shoulders with Christians, Mozarabs, and other Jews still deeply conditioned by the attitudes of the Islamic world. These, therefore, had every practical reason to set a high value on that culture which provided a common coin and a convertible currency.

Personal idiosyncracy touches every controversy. Unfortunately, the tendency within Jewish life has been to avoid biography and to argue the logical rather than the emotional issue. The young, zealous Meir chose resurrection, but was it really Maimonides' views which troubled him? Given the traditional freedom of Jewish dogmatics, this must be considered doubtful. What was at stake was Meir's whole context of religious values. No one likes to hear that what he holds most sacred is only the inferior part of a greater whole. Conversely, what excited Sheshet's ire? Certainly not a few *halachic* criticisms of the *Mishneh Torah* by a young whippersnapper. There is no indication that Sheshet idolized Maimonides. But one can imagine this cultivated physician and gentleman, who fancied himself as something of a scholar, rubbing shoulders with his equals at Pedro II's court happily agreeing that God's unity was Judaism's cardinal truth and, yes, that this belief was quite like the metaphysical ideas expressed by the best minds of the Islamic and Christian worlds. Sheshet could dismiss the uniqueness of Judaism as irrelevent. Jewish thought insisted on the existence of the one God. To doubt that Judaism's God was identical with the universally acknowledged philosopher's God was to doubt the rationalization which established Sheshet as an equal in his own eyes.

## References and Notes

1. *KTR*, III, 6a–7a — especially 6b.

2. *KTR*, III, 7a.

3. *KTR*, III, 6b.

4. J. Saracheck, *Faith and Reason* (Williamsport, 1935), p. 47; cf. H. Graetz, *A History of the Jews* (Philadelphia, 1894), III, 524, "His hostile attitude toward science and his tendency towards an ossified Judaism, isolated him even in his own circle."

5. The author can not adequately render this verse.

6. H. Brody, "Poems and Letters of Meir ha-Levi Abulafia" (Heb.), *Yedeot ha-Mahon Le-Heker ha-Shira ha-Ivrit,* II (Berlin, 1936), 32–35, No. 12. The author's translation.

7. These "cursed days" probably referred to the early 13th century Almohade incursion in Andalusia which threatened Meir's home in Toledo, but they might also refer to the brewing Albigensian Crusade which as early as 1209 had decimated the Jewish community of Béziers.

8. I. Baer, *A History of the Jews of Spain* (Philadelphia, 1961), I, 96.

9. *KTR*, III, 7a.

10. Zerahyah ha-Yevani, *Sefer ha-Yashar* (Vienna, 1811), V. This work was for a time erroneously ascribed to Jacob b. Meir, Rabbenu Tam.

11. Joseph Albo, *Sefer ha-Ikkarim*, I. Husik (ed., trans.) (Philadelphia, 1929), i. 15.134–5.

12. H. A. Wolfson, *Philo* (Cambridge, 1947), I, 396 ff. Compare the Talmudic treatment of Deut. 32:39, "I kill and I make alive," as a proof text of resurrection

(*T. B. Sanhedrin* 91b) and Philo's use of Gen. 15:15, "But thou shalt go to thy fathers nourished with peace, in a goodly old age" as a proof text of the immortality of the soul. (Philo, *Quaestiones et Solutiones in Genesim* 3:11, quoted in Wolfson, I, 398.)

13. *T. B. Baba Batra* 16a.

14. Eccl. 3:19 ff.; *Ben Sira* 41:3 ff.

15. Dan. 12:1–4 was often cited as Scriptural authority for this tenet. Cf. Isa. 26:19, Job. 14:13–15. But the promise was nowhere insisted upon in the Torah law.

16. *M. T. Teshubah* 8:2.

17. Meir Abulafia, *Kitab al Rasail,* Y. Brill (ed.) (Paris, 1871), p. 14.

18. *T. B. Berachot* 17a.

19. Meir Abulafia, p. 14.

20. *Ibid.*

21. Meir Abulafia, p. 15.

22. *M. T. Berachot* 1:11, *Shabbat* 20:7 and 2:11, *Milah* 3:6, *Tefillin* 1:11, and *Issure Bi'ah* 15:2.

23. *M. T. Abodah Zarah* 2:7, 4:2–4, *Mumar* 4:3.

24. *M. T. Kiddush ha-Hodesh* 4:16.

25. Meir Abulafia, p. 16.

26. *Ibid.*

27. *Ibid.,* p. 34.

28. *Ibid.,* p. 34.

29. *Ibid.,* p. 31.

30. *Ibid.,* p. 30.

31. *Ibid.,* p. 30.

32. *Ibid.,* p. 37.

33. *Ibid.,* p. 39.

34. *Ibid.,* p. 36.

35. *Ibid.,* p. 30.

36. *Ibid.,* p. 30.

37. *Ibid.,* p. 30.

38. *Ibid.,* p. 33.

39. *Ibid.,* p. 35.

40. *Ibid.,* p. 35.

41. *Ibid.,* pp. 36–37. Cf. Saadya Gaon, *The Book of Belief and Opinions,* trans. S. Rosenblatt (New Haven, 1948), pp. 264–289, and the variant text pp. 409–435.

42. Meir Abulafia, p. 37.

43. *Ibid.,* p. 37.

44. *Ibid.,* p. 45 ff.

45. *TR,* 52.

46. *T. B. Ketubot* 29a.

47. In cases where Maimonides decided between two well defended decisions, as in the case of *M. T. Abodah Zarah* 2:7 (concerning the special name of God which if uttered constituted blasphemy) Aaron simply took the offensive: "How can you think that he erred, behold our master recognized both opinions, since he specifically quoted the variant . . . It is evident that he went to the heart of the matter and chose the one which he found fit and proper. He weighed the issue in his understanding and in the scale of his knowledge." (Meir Abulafia, p. 47).

48. Meir Abulafia, p. 67.

49. *Ibid.,* p. 105.

50. *Ibid.,* p. 58.

51. *Ibid.,* pp. 97–98.

52. *Ibid.,* p. 51.

53. *Ibid.*

54. *Ibid.,* p. 57.

55. Saadya, pp. 414–417. Saadya had ruled that the literal version of a Biblical text may be questioned only when 1) it obviously conflicts with common sense experience, 2) it posits anthropomorphic attributes of God, 3) on the face of it there is an obvious error, or 4) authoritative interpretation had modified the apparent meaning.

56. Meir Abulafia, p. 52.

57. *Ibid.,* p. 52.

58. *Ibid.,* p. 53.

59. *Ibid.,* p. 54.

60. *Ibid.,* p. 54.

61. *Zohar,* iii. 152a, "The jar is not the wine, so stories do not make up the Torah."

62. Meir Abulafia, p. 56.

63. *Ibid.*

64. *Ibid.*

65. *Ibid.*

66. *Ibid.,* p. 2.

67. *Ibid.,* p. 7.

68. *Ibid.*

69. *Ibid.*

70. The list was abbreviated. *M. T. Kiddush ha-Hodesh* 4:16 and *Abodah Zarah* 2:4, among other issues of the Aaron correspondence, were missing.

71. "I do not care to argue with the great master after his death." (Meir Abulafia, p. 131.)

Gross developed what is known of Simson's life. His dates are uncertain. He was a younger contemporary of R. Isaac b. Samuel and R. Tam. He wrote commentaries to the Mishnah and the Sifre and was quoted in many responsa and in the Tosaphistic literature. He knew no Arabic. Of his pilgrimage to Palestine, more later. (H. Gross, "Étude sur Simson b. Abraham de Sens," *REJ,* VI [1883], 167–186; VII[1884], 40–47.)

72. Meir Abulafia, p. 107.

73. *Ibid.,* p. 108.

74. Simson based this on Num. 18:28, "Ye shall give the *Terumah* of God to Aaron the priest." The *Terumah* was given only in the Holy Land. The Bible can only mean that Aaron lives on, since he never entered Palestine. (Meir Abulafia, pp. 108–109.) cf. *T. B. Sanhedrin* 90b. cf. also Isa. 4:13, "And it shall come to pass that he that is left in Zion shall be called holy even any one that is written unto life in Jerusalem." Holy things never die.

75. Meir Abulafia, p. 135.

76. *Ibid.,* p. 131.

77. M. Higger, "Abraham ben Nathan Ha-Yarhi," *JQR,* XXXIV (1943), 342.

78. Cf. p. 117, note 2, above.

79. Meir Abulafia, p. 132.

80. *Ibid.,* p. 126.

81. *Ibid.,* pp. 131–132.

82. *Ibid.,* p. 149.

83. Saracheck, p. 60.

84. Abraham Maimonides, *Milhamot Adonai,* pp. 53–54.

85. Abraham Zacuto, *Sefer Yuhasin,* H. Filipowski (ed.) (London, 1857), p. 218.

86. Abraham Maimonides, *Milhamot Adonai,* p. 54.

87. Meir Abulafia, p. 106.

88. Higger, p. 330 ff.

89. Abraham b. Nathan ha-Yarhi, *Sefer ha-Minhag* (Berlin, 1855), p. 95.

90. Higger, pp. 342–346.

91. *Ibid.,* p. 348.

92. *Ibid.,* p. 348.

93. Interestingly, despite his critical position Abraham became in some way dependent on Meir. Brody has published a letter from Meir to certain citizens of Narbonne pleading that that commune release Abraham from taxes. (Brody, II [1936], 23, No. 9)

94. Graetz was the first to insist on the identity of these two names. (H. Graetz, *Geschichte der Juden von den Altesten Zeiten bis auf die Gegenwart,* 3rd ed. [Leipzig, 1894], III, 328.) Marx denied the identity but without offering proof. (Marx, *JQR,* XXV [1934], 408.) Baer showed that Sheshet b. Isaac lived in both Saragossa and Barcelona and concluded that the two names referred to one and the same man. "Er (Sheshet b. Benveniste of Barcelona) ist also wohl identisch mit "ששת בר יצחק בר יוסף בן בנשת סרקסתי" (Baer, *Die Juden* I, 35, note.) Brody questioned this identification on the basis of the close ties evidenced in a letter and

poem of condolence sent by Meir to Sheshet b. Isaac on the death of his son Samuel. (Brody, II, 61 and II, 88) However, family ties sometimes only acerbate a particular issue. The manuscript identification remains. Notice also the curious phrasing of the opening of Brody No. 39 where Meir seems to be alluding gently to Sheshet's dependence on reason and on knowledge (*Mada*) as a source of strength which ought not now desert him. (*Ibid.,* II, 88)

95. Marx, *JQR,* XXV (1934), 416–417, v. 75.

96. *Ibid.,* p. 417, vv. 97 ff.

97. At the close of his letter Sheshet reported the anger of a Castilian judge towards the *Mishneh Torah* (*Ibid.,* p. 365 ff.). Ostensibly this worthy's criticism was to Maimonides' method, his lack of citations, etc. — but Sheshet saw this critique not as a matter of judicial judgment but as an expression of peeve. Until the *Mishneh Torah* trained *halachists* had had things pretty much their way. Only a very few controlled even a limited competence in Talmudic jurisprudence. No one could dispute or challenge a judge's edict. Now such powers could be circumscribed. Everyone and anyone could check a decision by simply referencing it in the *Mishneh Torah.* There was an element of anti-rabbinic feeling in this. The *halachist* commanded authority by virtue of what was to the average Jew esoteric knowledge. Now that Maimonides had made the law an open book this preferential treatment was threatened. (*Ibid.,* p. 427) Had this hofjuden found his sway over Aragonese Jewry circumscribed by popular reverence for rabbinic authority and by rabbinic insistence on traditional norms?

Compare also the basis of Sheshet's structural attack on the office of the Rabbi-Judge to Meir's deep concern with judicial probity and competence.

"Today, the faithful are forced down into Sheol while they
(the times) hasten to exult the traitorous.
When I ask, what and why is this that the ends of the earth
should tremble from the rod of their wickedness
They answer me, with whom do you quarrel. Ask the judges who
pervert judgment.
They rig the scales of justice and cast off truth."
(Brody, II, 22, No. 5)

98. Marx, *JQR,* XXV (1934), 420, vv. 164–165.

99. *Ibid.,* p. 422, v. 234.

100. *Ibid.,* p. 419, vv. 144 ff.

101. *Ibid.,* p. 421, v. 198.

102. *Ibid.,* p. 420, v. 175.

103. *Ibid.,* pp. 420–421, vv. 191–197.

104. *Ibid.,* p. 426, vv. 356–358.

105. *Ibid.,* p. 424, v. 292.

106. *Ibid.,* p. 418, v. 108.

107. *Ibid.,* p. 425, vv. 312 ff.

108. *Ibid.,* p. 426, v. 362.

109. *Ibid.,* p. 427, vv. 360 ff.

110. *Ibid.,* p. 425, vv. 325 ff.

111. *Ibid.,* p. 422, vv. 231 ff.

112. *Ibid.,* p. 425, vv. 331 ff.

113. *Ibid.,* p. 414, vv. 2–3, p. 423, 312, 323.

114. *Ibid.,* p. 422, vv. 236 ff.

115. *Ibid.,* p. 426, v. 341. He based himself, however, on a proof text, "Open Thou mine eyes that I may behold wondrous things out of Thy law." (Ps. 119:18)

116. *Ibid.,* p. 414, vv. 10ff.

117. *Ibid.,* p. 414, vv. 12 ff.

118. H. Graetz, *Leket Shoshanim* (Breslau, 1862), p. 149; M. Steinschneider, "Moreh Mekom ha-Moreh," No. 11. Note, however, I. Davidson, *Thesaurus of Medieval Hebrew Poetry* (New York, 1924), I, 354, No. 7811. "It is difficult to decide who is the author."

119. H. Graetz, *Leket Shoshanim,* p. 149; M. Steinschneider, "Moreh Mekom ha-Moreh," No. 64.

120. Brody, II, 80, No. 34, vv. 13–15.

# Maimonides' Treatise on Resurrection
## Bibliography of Editions, Translations and Studies
### Revised Edition**
### By
### Jacob I. Dienstag

רשימה ביבליוגרפית זו של מאמר תחיית המתים היא חלק מביבליוגרפיה מקיפה של כל חיבורי הרמב"ם ומשנתו. החלק על ביאור מילות ההגיון, הופיע ב„ארשת", ספר ב' (תש"ך); על אגרת תימן, שם, ספר ג' (תשכ"א); על ספר המצוות, שם, ספר ה' (תשל"ב); על משנה תורה, בספר היובל לכבוד קיוב (תשל"ב) מתרגמים נוצרים של המשנה תורה ללאטינית, בספר היובל לכ' שלום ברון (תשל"ה); אגרת השמד או מאמר קידוש השם, קרית ספר, כרך נו, חוברת ב' (ניסן תשמ"א).

לא הסתפקתי ברישום המהדורות השונות של מאמר תחיית המתים וברישום המחקרים על המאמר, אלא אספתי וליקטתי גם את המובאות שמצאתי בכתבי חכמים מימה"ב. התוכן:

א.  מאמר תחיית המתים, מקור ותרגום*: מס' 1‎־29.
ב.  על מאמר תחיית המתים בספרות ימי הביניים: מס' 30‎־46.
ג.  מאמרים ומחקרים בעברית: מס' 47‎־65.
ד.  מאמרים ומחקרים בלועזית: מס' 66‎־82.
ה.  ציונים ביבליוגרפיים לכתבי־יד של מאמר תחיית המתים: מס' 83‎־114.

## A. Treatise on Resurrection — Text and Translation

שכ"ט 1569

[1] מאמר תחית המתים להרמב"ם ז"ל ומכתב התחיה להרב ר' יהודה זברא ז"ל. (קושטאנדינה), [דפוס שלמה בן יצחק יעבץ], (שכ"ט). [56] דף. °8.

דף [2]: דברי המדפיס.

דף [51]: קולופון: היתה השלמת הדפסת הספר הזה י"ג לאדר שנת חמשת אלפים ושכט לבריאת עולם פה קושטאנדינה. מבוא שערים [=תוכן שערי הספר]; דברי ר' יהודה

בכ"ר אברהם זארקון ושיר בשבח הספר ממנו הפותח: „זמן ביום גלה, יקר תבל כלה" (דאווידסון, אוצר השירה והפיוט, ב', עמ' 218, מס' 226) בהם נאמר, שכתבי־היד של שני הספרים היו בידי שם טוב ז' מינייר והוא שהביאם לדפוס: „ויאמר בלבו לצרפם במצרף שכלו ותקן עוותים ... ועל ספר שמם חקוקים וחרותם." על שינויים טיפוגרפיים בקצת טפסים, עיין י. ריבקינד, קרית ספר, ב (תרפ"ה‎־תרפ"ו), עמ' 63. ועיין א. יערי: הדפוס העברי בקושטא, ירושלים תשכ"ז, עמ' 115, מס' 175.

* התרגום העברי הוא מר' שמואל ז' תבון חוץ ממס' 25, 28, 29, 29.ב.
** המהדורה הקדמת הופיעה ב„קרית ספר", מח (תשל"ג), עמ' 730‎־740.

שפ"ט 1629

[2] מאמר תחיית המתים לרמב"ם. בתוך:
"לקוטים ... מהספר ... תעלומות חכמה
... [מאת] רבי יוסף (שלמה) מקנדיאה
[דילמדיגו] ...,", [חלק ב]. (בסיליאה,
שפ"ט). דף קד ע"א — קי ע"ב. 8°.

ת"ך 1660

[3] ספר המצות שחבר ... רבנו משה בן
מימון ... ובסוף החבור ראינו להדפיס אגרת
תימן ומאמר תחית המתים, שני חבורי הרב.
אמשטרדם, יוסף עטיאש, **ויאמר להם משה**
[ת"ך]. קלא דף. 4°.
דף קכח-קלא: מאמר תחיית המתים.

תנ"א 1691

[4] ספר תחיית המתים מהנשר ... רבינו
משה בר מימון ... ובתוכו ימצא תשובה
למינים האומרים אין תחית המתים מן
התורה ... פירדא, צבי הירש בן יוסף סג"ל,
שנת ויאמר ה' **אל משה הנך שוכב עם**
**אבותיך** וקם לפ"ק [תנ"א 1691]. ח דף. 8°.
קולופון: נעשה היום ג' י"ט מנחם תנ"א לפ"ק.

תע"ה 1715

[5] מאמר תחיית המתים מהנשר ... רבינו
משה בר מיימון ... תשובה למינים
האומרים אין תחיית המתים מן התורה ...
וגם ... ספר אגרת תימן ... נידפס ...
באותיות אמשטרדאם ... העונא, י"י
באסאנג, לסדר ולפרט הלמתים תעשה פלא
[תע"ה]. יג [צ"ל:כ] דף. 8°.
דף ב-ח: מאמר תחיית המתים.

תקכ"ב 1761

[6] באור מלות ההגיון להנשר ... רבינו
משה בר מימון ... ומאמר תחית המתים
להרמב"ם ... הובאו לדפוס על ידי ...

שמשון הקלירי ... פראנקפורט דאדר,
בדפוס דוקטור גרילו, תקכ"ב, [3], לו דף.
4°.
דף ל-לו: מאמר תחיית המתים. הפנים מנוקד.
על הוצאה זו של באור מלות ההגיון בהשמטת שם
המפרש של מנדלסון, עיין: י. י. דינסטאג, "מלות
ההגיון בתקופת ההשכלה", הדאר, שנה לד, גליון
כב (ט' ניסן תשט"ו), עמ' 420-422; י. י. דינסטאג,
"ביאור מלות ההגיון להרמב"ס", ארשת, ב
(תש"ך), עמ' 10, מס' 4.

תקכ"ט 1769

[7] מאמר תחיית המתים. בתוך: "ספר
הפדות והפורקן לרבינו סעדיה (גאון)".
אלטונא, [ר' יעקב עמדן], פרט של תקכ"ט.
דף יט, ב-כו. 8°. עם הקדמת ר' יעקב עמדן.
עיין: י. רפאל, כתבי ר' יעקב עמדין —
ביבליוגרפיה, ארשת, ג (תשכ"א), עמ' 272, מס'
ל'.

תקנ"ז 1794

[8] ספר הפדות והפורקן לר' סעדי' גאון
ז"ל מעיר אפיס וספר אגרת תימן וספר
מאמר תחיית המתים ... נדפס בראשונה על
תבנית הזאת ע"י הגאון ... יעב"ץ זלה"ה
וכעת נתעוררתי אני יהונתן בעל מדפיס
לעורר לבבות אחינו להביאו על מכבש
הדפוס פעם שנית ... דובנא, בדפוס
המשותפים יהונתן בהרמ"י ומיכל
פיאטראווסקי, תקנ"ד. 8°.
אותיות רש"י ובלא פאגינציה.

ת"ר 1840

[9] מאמר תחיית המתים ... הובא לבית
הדפוס ... ע"י מוה' נתנאל דוד בהרבני ...
מוה' משה צבי הלוי [זיסבערג] ... ווארשא,
דפוס דוד בן אריה ליב שקלאווער, ת"ר. יב
דף. 16°.

תרי"ח 1858

[10] מאמר תחיית המתים להרב ... משה
בר מיימון ... אשר חבר נגד ... הכופרים
בתחי' ... ובקשו להם מקלוט מחבוריו ...
לסלף דברי צדיקים כאלו הוא ... עומד ...
ח"ו לימינם ... [ווארשא], בדפוס צבי יעקב
באמבערג, שנת לחיותנו כהיום הזה [תרי"ח].
12 דף. °12. בשער גם: War[szawa],
Druk H. Bomberg, 1858.

תרי"ט 1859

[11] מאמר תחיית המתים. בתוך: „קובץ
תשובות הרמב"ם ואגרותיו", חלק ב. לפסיא,
פרט של תרי"ט. דף ז ע"ב — יא. °8.
דפוס צלום מזה, עיין להלן מס' 26.
א. א. הרכבי עמד על השינויים בין הוצאה זו
ודפוס קושטאנדינה שכ"ט (עיין להלן מס' 72).

תר"ך 1859

A discourse on the resurrec- [12
tion of the dead, translated by
S[abato] Morais. In: Jewish Messenger, vol. 6 (1859)' nos 11–15, p.
82–83, 90–91, 98, 106, 114.
תרגום אנגלי על יסד תרגום ר' שמואל ן' תיבון.

תרמ"ו 1886

[13] מאמר תחיית המתים להרב רבינו משה
בר מיימון ז"ל אשר חבר נגד האנשים ...
הכופרים בתחית המתים ... ה[ו]צאתיו לאור
מחדש מתוקן כראוי עפ"י כת"י הרב ...
ברך דברזהץ ... יצא לאור ע"י יוסף צבי
מאלימזאהן ... ושותפו אהרן בהרב ... ר'
דובערוש הכהן צייטלין, לונדון, חש"מ, שנת
משוש לפ"ק [=תרמ"ו]. י"ג דף. °12.
מתוך מעטפת הספר, שבידי נפתלי בן מנחם
נרשם גם בקטלוג הישן של הסמינר בניו יורק
לפני השרפה.

תרע"ב 1912

[14] מאמר תחיית המתים ומאמר קידוש
השם להרמב"ם ז"ל. מאמר האמונה ומאמר
הגאולה להרמב"ן ז"ל. יצא לאור מאת
מחזיקי הדת בווארשא ... ועם הוספות
ותיקונים מאת ... שלמה האלפרין נ"י נכד
בעל מגן אברהם ... הובא לביהד"פ ...
ע"י ר' משה ליפשיטץ ... בילגורייא, בדפוס
נתן נטע קראננענבערג, תרע"ב. 31 עמ'. °8.
עמ' 12־23: מאמר תחיית המתים.

תרע"ד 1914

[15] מאמר תחיית המתים ומאמר קידוש
השם להרמב"ם ז"ל. ... Варшава, Тип.
31 ,Г. Пимента и. я. Швабе, 1914
עמ'. °8.
בשער גם: בילגורייא, דפוס נתן נטע קראננענבערג,
תרע"ב 1912. ד"ס של הוצאה זו.

תרפ"ז 1927

[16] מאמר תחיית המתים. בתוך: „אגרות
ותשובות לרבינו משה בן מימון הספרדי
<הרמב"ם>". ורשה, „טרקלין", תרפ"ז.
ספירת עמודים שלישית: [1] ד', 1, [ג] —
כד עמ'. °8.
[1] ד': מבוא לאגרת מאת י.א. [יהודה אייגס],
(לפענוח ראשי התיבות, עיין הערתו של ג. אלקושי
בתוך: עלי ספר, ג', תשל"ז, עמ' 167). בדפוסים
הסטראוטיפיים של מהד' זו (להלן מס' 21, 23, 27)
נשמט המבוא הנ"ל.
ד"צ של הוצ' זו, בשינוי השם, עיין להלן מספר
19.

ת"ש 1939

[17] מאמר תחיית המתים.
Maimonides' Treatise on Resurrec-
tion <Maqala fi Ṭehiyyat Ha-
Metim>. The original Arabic and
Samuel ibn Tibbon's Hebrew trans-

lation and glossary. Edited with
critical apparatus notes and introduction by Joshua Finkel. New
York, American Academy for Jewish
Research, (typ. Press of the Jewish
Publication Society, Philadelphia),
1939. [2] p.l., p. 61–105; 38, 38*,
39–42, [5] p., 2 facsims. 8°.

שער נוסף: מקאלה פי תחית המתים; מאמר
תחית המתים. במקורו הערבי ובתרגום
שמואל אבן תבון ובצרוף פרושו לקצת מלים
בהעתקה עם מבוא והערות ושנויי נוסחאות.
ערוך עפ"י כתבי יד ודפוס ראשון ע"י יהושע
פינקל. ניו יורק, האקדמיה האמריקנית
למדעי היהדות, ת"ש. בתוך: Proceedings
of the American Academy for
Jewish Research, vol. ix (1939).

התוכן: מבוא (105־61). נוסח ערבי (1*־38*).
נוסח עברי (1־38), באור קצת מלות להר"ש ן'
תבון (39־42). על מהד' זו, עיין להלן מס' 49.
18 תדפיס מהנ"ל עם שינויים קלים
בפאגינציה ובתוספת דף ההקדשה (לדוב רבל) ודף
התיקונים.

### תש"ה 1945

[19] מאמר תחיית המתים. בתוך: "קובץ
מאמרי הרמבם', תשובות ... אודות עיקרי
אמונתנו הק'". ניו־יארק, "ישורון", תש"ה.
[1] דף, כד עמ'. 8°.
ד"צ מוגדל מאגרות ותשובות להרמב"ם, ורשה,
תרפ"ז (עיין לעיל מס' 16).

### תשי"א 1951

[20] אגרת או מאמר תחית המתים. בתוך:
"אגרות הרמב"ם', כרך ראשון ... בצירוף
... מבואות הכוללים יחד תולדות הרמב"ם
... יצירותיו ופעולותיו, ערוכות ומבוארות
על ידי מ[רדכי] ד[ב] רבינוביץ". תל־אביב,
"ראשונים", תשי"א. עמ' קצה־שצד. 8°.

---

התוכן: "פתח דבר" (קצג־ריג). "מבוא" הכולל
תולדות הרמב"ם (ריד־שלח). תוכן הפרקים
(שלט־שמ). מאמר תחיית המתים מנוקד ובאור
(שמא־שצג). שיר על תגמולי הנפשות בעולם
הנשמות לר' משה ן' עזרא (שצד). "את האגרת
הזאת ... ערכנו ... עפ"י הוצ' ה"קובץ" לפסיא,
אולם ... זכתה להוצאה מדעית־בקרתית מוגהת
ומתוקנת, מוארת בהערות ומעוטרת ... ע"י ...
יהושע פינקל [לעיל מס' 17] ... ועל פיה הגהנו
את הוצאתנו הנוכחית ..." (עמ' ריג).

### תשי"ד 1954

[21] מאמר תחיית המתים. בתוך: "אגרות
ותשובות להנשר הגדול רבינו משה בן מימון
הספרדי <הרמב"ם>". ירושלים, לוין־
אפשטין, [תשי"ד], ספירת עמ' שלישית: כד
עמ'.
ד"ס של הוצ' ורשה תרפ"ז בהשמטת המבוא מאת
י. א. [יהודה אייגס] (עיין לעיל מס' 16).

### תש"ך 1960

[22] אגרת או מאמר תחית הרמב"ם.
בתוך: "אגרות [הרמב"ם]", ערוכות ומבוארות
בצרוף מבואות מאת מ. ד. רבינוביץ. מהד' ב.
ירושלים, מוסד הרב קוק, תש"ך. עמ' קצה־
שצד. 8°.
זהה למהד' א (עיין לעיל מס' 20).

### תשכ"א 1961

[23] מאמר תחיית המתים. בתוך: "אגרות
ותשובות להנשר הגדול רבינו משה בן מימון
הספרדי <הרמב"ם>". ירושלים, לוין־
אפשטין, תשכ"א. ספירת עמודים שלישית:
כד עמ'. 8°.
ד"ס של הוצ' ורשה תרפ"ז, בהשמטת המבוא
מאת י. א. [יהודה אייגס] (עיין לעיל מס' 16).

### תשכ"ד 1964

[24] אגרת או מאמר תחית המתים. בתוך:
"אגרות הרמב"ם" ערוכות ומבוארות בצרוף

מבואות מאת מ. ד. רבינוביץ. ירושלים,
מוסד הרב קוק, תשכ"ד. עמ' קצה־שצד. °8.
ד"ס של הוצ' תש"ך (עיין לעיל מס' 22).

### תשכ"ו 1966

[25] איגרת תחית המתים. בתוך: „אגרות
אקטואליות של רבינו משה בן מימון
הספרדי. תורגמו/עובד ע"י מ. בר־יוסף".
חלק א. בני־ברק, מכון למדעי יהדות
[=מכון מרדכי להוצאת ספרי יהדות],
[תשכ"ו?]. °4. ספירת עמודים שלישית: [1]
ד', 16 עמ'.
פאראפרזה מתורגם ר"ש ז' תבון, „מיועד לקוראי
ימינו". משוכפל.

### תשכ"ז 1967

[26] מאמר תחיית המתים. בתוך: „אגרות
קנאות. אגרות הרמב"ם". ירושלים, תשכ"ז.
עמ' 7־11.
ד"צ מתוך „קובץ תשובות הרמב"ם ואגרותיו",
חלק ב, לפסיא, תרי"ט (עיין לעיל מס' 11).

### תשכ"ח 1968

[27] מאמר תחיית המתים. בתוך: „אגרות
ותשובות" להנשר . . . רבינו משה בן מימון
. . . ירושלים, לוין־אפשטיין, תשכ"ח. ספירת
עמ' שלישית: [1] ד', [ג]־כד עמ', °8.
ד"ס של הוצ' ורשה תרפ"ז, בהשמטת המבוא
מאת י. א. [יהודה אייגס] (עיין לעיל מס' 16).

### תש"ל 1970

[28] איגרת תחיית המתים. בתוך: „רבינו
משה בן מימון — איגרותיו ותולדות חייו"
[בעריכת מרדכי בר־יוסף]. (תל־אביב, מכון

מרדכי להוצאת ספרי יהדות, תש"ל), עמ'
72־92.
תרגום „בעברית המדוברת בימינו", בלוית „תוכן
העניינים בראשי פרקים" והערות.

### תשל"ב 1972

[29] מאמר בתחית המתים >מאמר תחית
המתים<, מקור ותרגום. בתוך: „רבינו משה
בן מימון, אגרות — מקור ותרגום, תירגם
לעברית, ביאר והכין על־פי כתבי יד ודפוסים
יוסף בכה"ר דוד קאפח". ירושלים, מוסד
הרב קוק, (תשל"ב 1972), עמ' סא־קא.

### תשל"ג 1973

Maimonides' Treatise on [א29
Resurrection. Translated from the
original Arabic with introduction
and notes by Milton Polinsky. MS
thesis, Yeshiva University, 1973. [1],
83 leaves. Typewritten.

### תש"ם 1981

[29ב] מאמר תחיית המתים בתרגומו של ר'
יהודה אלחריזי. יוצא לאור ע"י אברהם
הלקין. קבץ על יד, סדרה חדשה, ספר ט'
(יט). ירושלים: מקיצי נרדמים, תש"ם, עמ'
129־150.

### תשמ"ב 1982

Moses Maimonides' Treatise [ג29
on Resurrection. Translated and
annotated by Fred Rosner. New
York: KTAV, 1982.

## B. The Treatise on Resurrection in Medieval Hebrew Literature

ב"ר נחמן. בתוך: „קובץ תשובות הרמב"ם
ואגרותיו", חלק ג. לפסיא תרי"ט. דף ו־ז.

[30] אבולעאפיא, מאיר הלוי: נוסח הכתב
ששלח ר' מאיר הלוי . . . להחכם ר' משה

חזר ונדפס בתוך: א) „אגרות קנאות. אגרות
הרמב"ם". ירושלים תשכ"ז. דף ר"ז. — ב)
„הפולמוס על כתבי הרמב"ם בפרובאנס ובספרד;
לקט מקורות לסמינריון של אברהם גרוסמן".
ירושלים, האוניברסיטה העברית בירושלים,
הפקולטה למדעי הרוח, החוג להיסטוריה של עם
ישראל, תשל"א. עמ' 22‎-23.

[31] הנ"ל: כתאב אלרסאייל, מתורגם
בעברית — ספר אגרות לרב רבינו מאיר
הלוי ז"ל ב"ר טודרוס הלוי ... מטולטולה
הנודע בשם אבואלעפיאה. נקבץ בו אגרת
מהרמ"ה לרבני ארץ צרפת, אוגרת בתוכה
העתק אגרת הראשונה ממנו לחכמי לוניל,
ואגרת תוכחות עם אגרת תשובות מרבנו
אהרן אליו ואגרת האחרונה ממנו אליהם.
אגרת א' להכריע ביניהם ואגרת ב' להשיג
מרבנו שמשון ב"ר אברהם. אגרת מרמ"ה
אל ר"ש. אגרת מר"ש לרמ"ה. אגרת מרמ"ה
לר"ש. נמצא בכתובים באוצר נחמד אשר
בנוה הגביר ... יוחזל גינצבורג ... יצא
לאור על ידי יחיאל בריי"ל. פאריש, י.
בריי"ל, תרל"א, [2], 21, קנב עמ'. 8°.
ד"צ של הנ"ל: א) ירושלים, תשכ"ז. — ב) בתוך:
„הפולמוס על כתבי הרמב"ם בפרובאנס ובספרד",
עמ' 1‎-8 (קטע).

הנ"ל: אגרת הרמ"ה לחכמי לוניל בענין
תחיית המתים. בתוך: „סנהדרי גדולה למסכת
סנהדרין", כרך א', נערך על ידי יעקב הלוי
ליפשיץ. ירושלים, מכון הרי פישל, תשכ"ח.
עמ' קסו‎-קסז.

שם, עמ' קסח‎-קפה: תשובות ר' אהרן ב"ר
משולם מלוניל ור' שמשון ב"ר אברהם משאנץ
ותשובת הרמ"ה לר' אהרן. נעתק מהוצאת פאריש
הנ"ל. ועיין להלן מס' 76, שם עמ' 47‎-65; מס'
77, שם עמ' 109‎-124.

[32] הנ"ל: יד רמ"ה על סנהדרין, דף צ'
ע"א.

[33] אברבנאל, יצחק: ראש אמנה, פרקים
ח', ט"ו.

---

אברבנאל מכנה את המאמר בשם „אגרת
התחייה", עיין דברי דוד קאססעל בהערותיו לס'
מאור עינים לר' עזריה מן האדומים, (להלן מס'
41).

[34] אברהם ב"ר שלמה: קטע מתוך כתב-
יד הפותח „וקאל רבי' משה בן מימון פי'
רסאלה" תחית המתים . . .". בתוך: המזכיר,
שנה 20 (1880), עמ' 64‎-65.

המחבר הי' מפרש המקרא, במחצית השניה של
המאה הי"ד, בארצות הקדם.

[35] אהרן בן משולם בן יעקב מלוניל: כתב
ששלח הרב . . . רבי אהרן ב"ר משלם לרב
מאיר הלוי. בתוך: „טעם זקנים", י"ל ע"י
אליעזר אשכנזי. פרנקפורט א. מ., תרט"ו
1854. ד' סו ע"ב — ע ע"א.

חזר ונדפס: א) בתוך: „קובץ תשובות הרמב"ם
ואגרותיו", חלק ג'. לפסיא תרי"ט. ד' י"א‎-י"ג. —
ב) ד"צ של הנ"ל, ירושלים תשכ"ז.

נדפס גם בתוך: א) „כתאב אלרסאייל" . . .
פאריש תרל"א. עמ' כה‎-כ"מ. ד"צ של הוצ' זו,
ירושלים תשכ"ז. — ב) ההד, שנה י, חוב' ז (ניסן
תרצ"ה), עמ' ח"ט. — ג) „תולדות ספרות
ישראל" מאת י. צינוברג, כרך א (תל אביב, יוסף
שרברק, 1955, עמ' 307‎-308). — ד) „הפולמוס
על כתבי הרמב"ם בפרובאנס ובספרד . . .".
ירושלים, תשל"א, ד' 4‎-8. ד"צ מתוך הוצ'
פאריש הנ"ל. — ה) „מבחר ספרות המחשבה
והמוסר בפרובאנס; חומר לסמינריון של ד"ר י.
דן". ירושלים, האוניברסיטה העברית, הפקולטה
למדעי הרוח, החוג לספרות עברית, תשל"א. ד'
1‎-6.

[35א] אלשקר, ר' משה: שאלות ותשובות.
סביוניטה, שי"ד; סדילקאב, תקפ"ד; ירושלים,
תשי"ט; סימן קיז; נדפס גם בפני עצמו בשם
„השגות שהשיג על מה שכתב רבי שם
טוב . . ." פירארא שי"ז/1556. (16 דף).

[36] בחיי ב"ר אשר: ביאור על התורה,
לדברים ל, טו (מהד' ד. שעוועל, כרך ג,
ירושלים תשכ"ח, עמ' תמד).

[37] דוראן, שמעון בן צמח: מגן אבות. ליוורנו, בדפוס אברהם יצחק קאשטילו, תקמ"ה 1785. ד' צב ע"א-ע"ב, צט ע"ב. ד"צ של הנ"ל: ירושלים [תשכ"ט?].

[38] משה בן מימון: תשובת הרמב"ם ז"ל למר יוסף בן גאבר מאנשי בגדד שנכללה בה שאלות. בתוך: חמדה גנוזה, ע"י צ. ה. עדעלמאן, מחב' א'. קניגסבערג תרט"ז. ד' ג ע"ב-ו ע"א.

„אבל מה ששמעת אותם אומרים שאנחנו הרחקנו תחיית המתים ר"ל חזרת נפש לגוף . . . וכבר חיברנו בזה העניין מאמר [תחיית המתים]". התשובה נדפסה גם בתוך: א) „טעם זקנים", י"ל ע"י אליעזר אשכנזי, פרנקפורט א. מ., תרט"ו 1854, ד' עג ע"ב-עו ע"א. ב) „קובץ תשובות הרמב"ם ואגרותיו", לפסיא תרי"ט, חלק ב, ד' טו ע"ג-טז ע"ד.

[39] הנ"ל: תשובות הרמב"ם, אספן . . . אברהם חיים פריימן. ירושלים, מקיצי נרדמים, תרצ"ד. עמ' 367; הוצאת י. בלאו, שם, תש"ך, עמ' 578.

רבינו מתייחס ל„מאמר תחיית המתים" בתשובה להשגותיו של ר' שמואל בר' עלי בעניין תחיית המתים.

[40] משה בן נחמן: שער הגמול. בסוף הספר מצטט הרמב"ן את המאמר ומתפלמס עם הרמב"ם (במהד' ח. ד. שעוועל של כתבי הרמב"ן, ירושלים תשכ"ד, עמ' שט-שיא).

[40א] הנ"ל: תורת ה' תמימה, הוצאת אהרן יילניק, תרל"ג, עמ' 14.

[41] עזריה מן האדומים: קטעים מתוך מאמר תחיית המתים. בתוך: „מאור עינים", חלק „אמרי בינה", פרק ג וסוף פרק ז. עיין במהד' דוד קאסטעל, ווילנא תרכ"ו, וכן הערות המהדיר בעמ' 93-94. ועיין גם: י. פינקל, מאמר תחיית המתים (לעיל מס' 17), עמ' 64, הערה 4.

[42] שלום, אברהם בן יצחק: נוה שלום.

קושטאנטינה רצ"ח, מאמר יא, פרק ח. יבאר בו המחלוקת שנפל בין הרמב"ם והרמב"ן במלת עולם הבא אם מיד אחר המות כדעת הרמב"ם אם בתחיית המתים כדעת הרמב"ן ומכריע כדברי הרמב"ם. חזר ונדפס: א) ויניציאה של"ה. ד' קצח. — ב) Farnborough 1969 ד"צ של הנ"ל.

[43] שמשון ב"ר אברהם משאנץ: תשובות לר' מאיר הלוי אבולעאפיה. בתוך: „כתאב אלרסאייל". פאריש תרל"א. עמ' קז-קמט. עיין להלן מס' 76, שם עמ' 58-60; שם 77, שם עמ' 124-128.

[44] ששת ב"ר יצחק הנשיא: כתב ששלח החכם הנשיא ר' ששת צבי הספרדי ושלחה לחכמי לוניל על אודות הכתב ששלח ר' מאיר ז"ל ממדינת אוליטולה בעניין תחיית המתים. בתוך: -H. Graetz, Ein hand schriftliches Schreiben des Sche-shcet Benvenist eüber Maimuni's Wirksamkeit, MGWJ, 25 (1876), p. 509-512; A. Berliner: Scheschet b. Isak, HB, 17 (1877), p. 65.

סיום ל„כתב הנ"ל, בתוך „חדשים גם ישנים" מאת אברהם אליהו הרכבי, מס' 10; ובתוך „דברי ימי ישראל" לצבי גראטץ, חלק ה, ורשה, האחים שולדבערג, תרנ"ז, עמ' 10-12 (ובדפוסים הסטראוטיפיים של הוצ' זו: ורשה, הוצאת אחיאסף", תרס"ט; ורשה, לוין-אפשטיין, תרס"ח; שם, הוצאת „אחיספר", חש"ד; שם, הוצאת „מרכז", חש"ד).

הכתב נדפס מחדש, עם תיקונים, על-ידי: -Alex ander Marx: Texts by and about Maimonides, JQR, N.S. 25 (1935), 428-406. ד"צ של הוצ' מארקס הנ"ל בהשמטת המבוא בתוך: „הפולמוס על כתבי הרמב"ם בפרובאנס ובספרד" (לעיל מס' 30), עמ' 9-16.

עיין: ג. שלום, ראשית הקבלה, ירושלים, הוצאת שוקן תש"ה, עמ' 133-134. ועיין גם: להלן מס' 76, שם עמ' 61-65; מס' 77, שם עמ' 128-135.

[45] תבון, שמואל ן': „ביאור קצת מלות

להר״ש ז׳ תבון באו בהעתקותיו", בסוף
„מאמר תחיית המתים" (לעיל מס׳ 17, עיין
בתוכן).

[46] תנחום ירושלמי: הקדמת ספר
אלמרשד אלכאפי (המדריך המספיק). תורגם
מערבית לעברית ע״י ברוך טולידאנו. בתוך:
סיני, כרך 44 (תשי״ט), עמ׳ קא [=ספר
אלמרשד אלכאפי, כרך א׳, תל־אביב,
תשכ״א].
מצטט את המאמר.

## C. Essays and Studies (Hebrew)

[47] אוריין, מאיר: המורה לדורות; רבינו
משה בן מימון. ירושלים, מוסד הרב קוק,
תשט״ז.
על מאמר תחיית המתים: עמ׳ 93־96.

[48] בנעט, דוד צבי: ר׳ יהודה אלחריזי
ושלשלת התרגומים של מאמר תחיית המתים
לרמב״ם. בתוך: תרביץ יא (ת״ש), עמ׳
260־270.
נגד י. זנה (עיין להלן מס׳ 55).

[49] הנ״ל: לנוסח מאמר תחיית המתים של
הרמב״ם ולתרגומו. בתוך: תרביץ יג (תש״ב),
עמ׳ 37־42.
הערות לנוסח הערבי והעברי בתרגומו של ר׳
שמואל ז׳ תיבון, בקשר למהדורתו של יהושע
פינקל (עיין לעיל מס׳ 17).
הדפסה מיוחדת של המאמר הנ״ל: ירושלים,
תש״ב. 6 עמ׳.

[50] ברט, א.: פולמוס הרמב״ם. בתוך:
בטרם, שנה 14, חוב׳ א (י״ז טבת תשט״ז),
עמ׳ 29־30.
נגד מאמרו של י. ליבוביץ „על הרמב״ם, על
אמונה ועל פולקלור" (עיין להלן מס׳ 60).

[51] ברמן, אליעזר זאב: מיתוס מדיני
וקנאות דתית חברתית. בתוך: „אבן באג׳ה
והרמב״ם"; פרק בתולדות הפילוסופיה
המדינית". דיס׳, ירושלים 1959. עמ׳
134־185 ועמ׳ xvi-xxix של הסיכום
האנגלי: Ibn Bājjah and Maimonides;
a chapter in the history of political
philosophy . . . by Lawrence Victor
Berman.

[52] גוטמן, יצחק יוליוס: הפילוסופיה של
היהדות. ירושלים, מוסד ביאליק, תשי״א.
עמ׳ 170־171.
חזר ונדפס: ירושלים, מוסד ביאליק, תשי״ג. עמ׳
170־171. ד״ס של ההוצ׳ הקדמת. המקור
הגרמני ותרגום אנגלי, ראה להלן מס׳ 70.

[53] הלברשטאם, שלמה זלמן חיים:
[מכתב לקלמן שולמן, אסרו חג שבועות
תרל״ג]. בתוך: „תולדות חכמי ישראל", מאת
קלמן שולמן, חלק ב. ווילנא, ראם תר״ם;
תרמ״ד; תרע״א, עמ׳ ix-x.
לדעת המחבר, ר׳ מאיר הלוי אבולעאפיא התנגד
לרמב״ם רק בעניין תחיית המתים בטרם ראה את
מאמר תחיית המתים.

[54] וייס, אייזק הירש: „תולדות הרב
רבינו משה בן מימון". בתוך: „בית תלמוד",
שנה א. וויען תרמ״א. עמ׳ 329־330 [=
„תולדות גדולי ישראל", עמ׳ 46־47].

[55] זנה, ישעיהו: אגרת הרמב״ם לשמואל
ז׳ תבון עפ״י טופס בלתי ידוע הנמצא
בארכיון הקהילה בוירונה. בתוך: תרביץ, י
(תרצ״ט), עמ׳ 152.
על שימושו של אלחריזי בתרגומו של ר׳ תיבון
למאמר תחיית המתים. ועיין: ד. צ. בנעט (לעיל
מס׳ 48).

[56] זק״ש, שניאור: בתוך: היונה, תרי״א,
עמ׳ 77.

[57] טייכר, יעקב ל.: זיוף ספרותי במאה
הי"ג — מאמר תחיית המתים של הרמב"ם.
בתוך: מלילה, קובץ א (מנצ'סטר, תש"ד),
עמ' 81-92.

"המאמר ,תחיית המתים' אינו פרי עטו של
הרמב"ם, אלא זיוף. הוא נתחבר לכתחילה
בעברית — לכל המוקדם במחיצת השניה של
המאה הי"ג, והנוסח העברי הופץ בין קהילות
ישראל בתור תרגום שמואל ן' תבון של המקור
הערבי כביכול של הרמב"ם . . ." (עמ' 92). על
מאמרו של טייכר, עיין: ש. ברוך, מחקרי יהדות
לחכמי אנגליה, "התקופה" ל-לא (תש"ו), עמ'
825-826. נגדו יצא י. זנה (עיין להלן מס' 78)
סיכום ביקורתו ניתנה ע"י י. יעקבוביץ, הדואר, א'
סיון תשי"ג, עמ' 530.


[58] כהנא, קלמן: "ספר הזכרון" לריטב"א,
יו"ל ע"י . . . ק. כהנא. ירושלים תשט"ז. עמ'
ז, כו-כז.
על בקיאות הרמב"ן במאמר תחיית המתים.


[59] לוצאטו, שמואל דוד: מכתב ליש"ר.
בתוך: כרם חמד, מחברת ג (תקצ"ח), עמ'
67-70.
נגד השקפתו של הרמב"ם על השארת הנפש
במאמר תחיית המתים.

הנ"ל: מי הוא מחבר המשנה ועל סדר
מסכתותיה ונגד הרמב"ם. בתוך: "פניני
שד"ל". פרעזעמישל תרמ"ח. עמ' 386-389.
הנ"ל: כתיבת המשנה והרמב"ם. בתוך:
"מחקרי יהדות", חלק ב, ורשה, תרע"ג, עמ'
166-169.
זהה לנ"ל.


[60] ליבוביץ, ישעיהו: על הרמב"ם, על
אמונה ועל פולקלור. בתוך: בטרם, שנה יג,
חוב' ט (ט"ז חשון תשט"ז), עמ' 21-22.
לדעת המחבר, מאמר תחיית המתים לא יצא מעטו

של הרמב"ם: איגרת זו "כולה סתירה משוועת
לכל מה שהגה הרמב"ם בכתביו האותנטיים".

[60א] ליפשיץ, יעקב הלוי: מבוא ללקט
איגרות הרמ"ה (על פסקי הרמב"ם בענייני
מס' סנהדרין). ב"סנהדרי גדולה למסכת
סנהדרין", כרך א'. ירושלים: הוצאת מכון
הרי פישל, תשכ"ח, עמ' 51-54.
על מאמר תחיית המתים בפולמוס בין הרמ"ה, ר'
אהרן ב"ר משולם מלוניל ור' שמשון משאנץ.


[61] עגנון, שמואל יוסף: אגרת תחיית
המתים להרמב"ם ז"ל. בתוך: "ספר סופר
וספור: סיפורים על סופרים ועל ספרים".
ירושלים, שוקן, תרצ"ח, עמ' סה.
אימרה מהבעש"ט על מאמר תחיית המתים.


[62] פינס, שלמה: מאמר תחיית המתים.
בתוך: "תולדות הפילוסופיה היהודית
מהרמב"ם עד שפינוזה; רשימות לפי
הרצאות, ערכה א. ברושי". ירושלים, מפעל
השכפול — בית ההוצאה של הסתדרות
הסטודנטים של האוניברסיטה העברית,
תשכ"ד. עמ' 42-44.


[63] קאפח, יוסף: הערות על ספר "בסתאן
אלעקול-גן השכלים" לר' נתנאל בירב פיומי.
ירושלים, האגודה להשכלת גנזי תימן,
(תשי"ד). עמ' קן, הערה 68.
רומז לזהות הרעיונות בין ספר זה והרמב"ם בסוף
"מאמר תחיית המתים", ומסכם: "ונראה הדבר
שהרמב"ם ראה את מאמרו הנ"ל".


[64] שולמן, קלמן: "תולדות חכמי
ישראל", חלק ב'. ווילנא, ראם, תר"ם;
תרמ"א; תרע"א. עמ' 62-63; 89; 97.


[65] שלום, גרשום: ראשית הקבלה.
ירושלים, שוקן, תש"ח. עמ' 133-135.
על הפולמוס הראשון בעניין תחיית המתים במחנה
המקובלים ביזמת ר' מאיר הלוי אבולעאפיה.

## D. Essays and Studies (non-Hebrew)

66] Bacher, Wilhelm: "Die Agada in Maimunis Werken". In: Moses Ben Maimon; sein Leben, seine Werke und sein Einfluss ... Hrsg. von der Gesellschaft zur Förderung der Wissenschaft des Judentums durch W. Bacher, M. Brann, D. Simonsen. Band II. Leipzig, G. Fock, 1914, p. 197.

66a] Baron, Salo Wittmayer: A Social and Religious History of the Jews, vol. VIII. New York: Columbia University Press, 1958, p. 308, note 4.

67] Dassovius, Theodorus: סוד תחיית המתים Diatribe, qua Judaeorum de resurrectione mortuorum sententia, ex plurimis ... Rabbinis ... explicatur, examinatur, et illustratur ... Wittebergae, Typis Matthaei Henckelii, 1675. 12 p.l., 208, [8] p. 8°.
2nd ed: [Wittebergae?], sumptibus J.C. Follgineri, 1693. [24], 208, [8] p. 8°.

67a] Dienstag, Jacob I[srael]: Introduction to his *Eschatology in Maimonidean Thought*. New York: KTAV, 1981, pp. xv-cxx.
Reflections on those personages associated with the scholarship of the *Treatise on Resurrection*.

67b] Dienstag, Jacob I[srael]: Eschatology in Maimonidean Thought: A Selected Bibliography. In: ibid.

68] Eisenmenger, Johann Andreas: Entdecktes Judenthum. Koenigsberg, 1711. Vol. 2: p. 890–950.
דעות חכמי ישראל בענין תחיית המתים ויחסם למאמר תחיית המתים מאת הרמב״ם. המחבר היה, כידוע, אנטישמי מפורסם.

68a] Goldfeld, Lea Naomi: An Inquiry into the Authenticity of Moses Maimonides' *Treatise on Resurrection*. New York: KTAV, 1982.

69] Finkel, Joshua: Maimonides' Treatise on Resurrection; a comparative study. In: Essays on Maimonides ... ed. by S.W. Baron. New York, Columbia University Press, 1941. p. 93–121.
Rev. by Max Wiener, Journal of Jewish Bibliography, vol. 3 (1942), p. 95.

70] Guttmann, Julius: Die Philosophie des Judentums. München, E. Reinhardt, 1933. p. 207.
Id.: Philosophies of Judaism, tr. by David W. Silverman. Philadelphia, Jewish Publication Society, 1964. p. 184.
תרגום עברי ראה לעיל מס׳ 52.

71] Halberstam, S[alomon] J[oachim]: Verbesserungen. In: Israelietische Leterbode, vol. 7 (1881–1882), p. 176.
תיקונים למבוא לתחיית המתים שהוציא נויבויער (להלן מס׳ 74).

72] Harkavy A.: Fragment einer Apologie des Maimonidischen מאמר

תחיית המתים. In: Zeitschrift fuer hebraeische Bibliographie, vol. 2 (1897), p. 125-128; 181-188.

נגד התקפתו של ר' שמואל בן עלי על שיטת הרמב"ם בעניין תחיית המתים. עיין: J.L. Teicher, Maimonides' letter to Joseph b. Jehudah, a literary forgery, Journal of Jewish Studies, 1 (1948), p. 43.

73] Kohler, Kaufmann: Resurrection. In: Jewish Encyclopedia, vol. 10 (1905), p. 384-385.

74] Neubauer, A[dolf]: Vorrede zu Maimonides' תחיית המתים, Ubers, von Jehudah ibn Thabbon. In: Israelietische Letterbode, vol. 7 (1881-1882), p. 99-101.

מתוך כ"י אוקספורד. שזח"ה (לעיל מס' 71) תיקן שצ"ל: אלחריזי — ולא יהודה ן' תיבון. חזר ונדפס ע"י י. פינקל בסוף מבואו למאמר תחית המתים (לעיל מס' 17). עפ"י דברי אלחריזי בהקדמתו תורגם מאמר תחה"מ לערבית, מתוך תרגומו של ר"ש תיבון, ע"י ר' יוסף בן יואל, כי לא ניתן היה להשיג את המקור הערבי בזמנו. מתוך תרגום ערבי זה — כותב אלחריזי — חזר ותירגם את המאמר לעברית. פינקל מטיל ספק באותנטיות של הקדמה זו (עיין מבואו, שם, עמ' 79-84). בעיה זו העסיקה גם את שטיינשניידר (המזכיר, 21, 1881, עמ' 134-135; העברעישע איבערזעטזוונגען, עמ' 431) וד"ץ בנעט (לעיל מס' 48).

75] Poznanski, Samuel: Samuel b. Ali ha-Lewi gen. Ibn Al-Dastur. In: "Babylonische Geonim im nachgaonäischen Zeitalter nach handschriftlichen und gedruckten Quellen". Berlin, Mayer & Mülter, 1914. p. 15-36.

על יחסם של ר' שמואל בן עלי, זכריה בן ברכאל, דניאל הבבלי לספרי הרמב"ם והשקפתו בעניין תחיית המתים. עיין: אגרות הרמב"ם, הוצאת ד. צ.

בנעט, חוב' א, ירושלים, "מקיצי נרדמים", תש"ו, עמ' 31-38; ש. אסף, קובץ של אגרות ר' שמואל בן עלי ובני דורו תרביץ א (תר"ץ) עמ' 107-108; J. Mann, Texts and Studies, vol. 1, Cincinnati, Ohio, 1931, p. 240-242.

76] Saracheck, Joseph: Faith and reason; the conflict over the rationalism of Maimonides. Williamsport, The Bayard Press, 1935.

77] Silver, Daniel Jeremy: Maimonidean criticism and the Maimonidean Controversy, 1180-1240. Leiden, E.J. Brill, 1965. Pp. 109-135 reprinted in J.I. Dienstag, ed. *Eschatology in Maimonidean Thought.* New York: KTAV, 1981 and in Moses Maimonides' *Treatise on Resurrection,* translated by F. Rosner. New York: KTAV, 1982.

78] Sonne, Isaiah: A scrutiny of the charges of forgergy against Maimonides' "Letter on Resurrection". In: Proceedings of the American Academy for Jewish Research, vol. xxi (1952), p. 101-117; reprinted in J.I. Dienstag, ed. *Eschatology in Maimonidean Thought.* New York: KTAV, 1981.

נגד י. ל. טייכר (לעיל מס' 57). סיכום ביקורת זו ניתנה ע"י י. יעקבוביץ. הדואר, א' סיון תשי"ג, עמ' 530; א. ש. הלקין, תרביץ כה (תשט"ז), עמ' 415.

78a] Steinschneider, Moritz: Maimonides. *Hebraeische Bibliographie,* 21 (1881), 134-135. See note on no. 74.

78b] Twersky, Isadore: Introduction to the Code of Maimonides *(Mishneh Torah)*. New Haven: Yale University Press, 1980, pp. 43-45. See also Index, pp. 640-641.

79] Waxman, Meyer: Maimonides as a dogmatist. In: Year Book Central Conference of American Rabbis, vol. 45 (1935), p. 414.

80] Weiss, Adolf: Mose ben Maimons Leben und Werke. In: "Mose ben Maimon, Führer der Unschlüssigen", ins deutschen übertragen ... von Adolf Weiss, I,

Leipzig, Felix Meiner, 1923, p. clvi-clx.

81] Wiener, Max: Auferstehung der Toten. In: Encyclopaedia Judaica, vol. 3, Berlin, (c 1929), col. 667.

82] Wolfson, Harry Austryn: Note on Maimonides' classification of the sciences. In: Jewish Quarterly Review, New Series, vol. 26 (1936), p. 373; reprinted in his *Studies in the History of Philosophy and Religion,* vol. I. Cambridge, Mass.: Harvard University Press, 1973, p. 555.

על המונח „האומה" ב„מאמר תחיית המתים".

## E. Bibliographical References to the Treatise on Resurrection
### (רובם לכתבי יד של המאמר).

[83 אלוני, נחמיה; דוד שמואל לוינגר: רשימות תצלומי כתבי־היד העבריים במכון [לתצלומי כתבי־היד העבריים בבית הספרים הלאומי והאוניברסיטאי]. חלק א: כה״י בספריות אוסטריה וגרמניה. ירושלים, משרד החינוך והתרבות — המכון לכתבי־היד העבריים, תשי״ז. מספר 530 (ג).

חלק ג: כתבי־היד שבספריית הווטיקן. ירושלים, ר. מס, תשכ״ח. מספר 251 (א).

[83א אלוני, נחמיה: רשימות ספרים עתיקות בווטיקאן. ארשת, ד' (תשכ״ו), עמ' 226.

[84 ברלינר, אברהם: מכתבים אשר הריצו החכמים צונץ ומיכאעל איש אל רעהו, הו״ל אברהם ברלינר. בתוך: Jahrbuch der jüdisch-literarischen Gesellschaft, (1906) iv, חלק עברי, עמ' 113, מכתב 56.

מיכל מודיע לצונץ אודות כתב היד של מאמר תחיית המתים שרכש לו.

[84א דויד, אברהם: תרגום בלתי ידוע לאגרת תחיית המתים לרמב״ם. קרית ספר, נג, חוברת ב' (ניסן תשל״ח), עמ' 377-378.

[84ב דינסטאג, ישראל יעקב: מאמר תחיית המתים להרמב״ם; ביבליוגראפיה של הוצאות, תרגומים ומחקרים. קרית ספר, כרך מח (תשל״ג), עמ' 730-740.

[84ג דינסטאג, ישראל יעקב: מאמר תחיית המתים להרמב״ם; ביבליוגראפיה של הוצאות, תרגומים ומחקרים. (מהדורה מתוקנת) ב-*Escha-*, .ed ,J. I. Dienstag *tology in Maimonidean Thought.* New York: KTAV, 1981 and in Moses Maimonides' *Treatise on Resurrection.* Translated by F. Rosner. New York: KTAV, 1982.

[85 זק״ש, שניאור: בית יוסף, הוא רשימה מכל הספרים היקרים כתבי יד הנמצאים

באוצר ... של הרב ... יוסף יוזל גינצבורג, מס' 45 (8); 360 (2).
במכון לתצלומי כתבי-היד העבריים בבית הספרים הלאומי והאוניברסיטאי נמצא צילום של הקטלוג הנ"ל.

[86] יאפ"ז [י. גולדבלום]: גנזי ישראל ברומי-רבתי. בתוך: בית עקד; מאסף מאמרים, שירים וספורים ... יו"ל ע"י ש"י איש הורוויץ, חוברת א', ברדיטשוב תרנ"ב. עמ' 19.

תיאור כ"י של מאמר תחיית המתים בספרית אנג'ליקא (Cod. A, 4, 14).
על התרגום הלטיני של מאמר תחיית המתים מאת המומר פלאוויוס מיתרידאטס, מורה1 בקבלה של פיקו דלה מירא נדולה. עיין עליו מחקריו של ח. וירשובסקי: פלאוויוס מיתרידאטס, בתוך: "דברי האקדמיה הלאומית הישראלית למדעים", כרך א, חוברת ג, ירושלים תשכ"ד; נוסח קדום של פירוש מורה נבוכים על דרך הקבלה לר' אברהם אבולעפיה בתרגומו הלאטיני של פלאוויוס מיתרידאטס, שם, כרך ג, חוברת ה, תשכ"ט.

---

87] Assemani, Stephanus Evodius et Joseph Simonius: Bibliothecae Apostolicae Vaticanae codicum manuscriptorum catalogus ... vol. I. Romae, 1756. No. ccxcii(1); ccciii(9); cccxl(4); Urbinates-Vaticani, no. xxiii(4).
בתרגום ר"ש ן' תבון. ד"צ של הקטלוג הנ"ל י"ל בפאריז 1926.

88] Bartolocci, Giulio: קרית ספר. בפר. והוא חבור גדול שבו נכתבו כל ספרי היהודים, חברו ויסדו ... יוליוס ברטולוקי Bibliotheca magna rabbinica de scriptoribus & scriptis hebraicis, Pars 4. Romae, 1693. p. 105.

89] Berliner, Abraham: Hebräische Handschriften in Mailand. In: Magazin f. die Wissenschaft des Judenthums, 7 (1880), p. 119 [=Gesammelte Schriften, I: Italien, Frankfurt a.M., J. Kaufmann, 1913, p. 118].

89a] Bernheimer, Carlo: Codices Hebraici Bybliothecae Ambrosianae descripti a ... Florentiae, 1933, no. 87 (13).

90] Capua, Angelo di: Catalogo dei codici ebraici della Biblioteca Angelica. Firenze, 1878. No. 13 (2).

91] Dukes, Leopold: Literaturblatt des Orients, XI (1850), col. 302.

92] Finkel, Joshua: Maimonides' Treatise on Resurrection, (see above no. 17), p. 87-92.

93] Freimann, Aaron: Union Catalog of Hebrew Manuscripts and their Locations, vol. 2. New York, American Academy for Jewish Research, 1964, p. 181, no. 4748.

94] Hirschfeld, Hartwig: Descriptive catalogue of the Hebrew mss. of the Montefiore library. London, Macmillan & Co. 1904, p. 93, no. 297 (5) [=Jewish Quarterly Review, vol. 14 (1902), p. 644]. Farnborough ד"צ של הקטלוג הנ"ל: 1969

95] Loewe, Herbert: Handlist of Hebrew and Samaritan Manuscripts in the Library of the University of Cambridge. Rev. and comp. by J.D.

Pearson and Raphael Lowe. No. 396 (Add. 491,2).

במכון לתצלומי כתבי היד בבית הספרים הלאומי והאוניברסיטאי נמצא צילום של הקטלוג הנ״ל.

96] Loewinger, David Samuel & Bernard Dov Weinryb: Catalogue of the Hebrew manuscripts in the Juedisch-Theologisches Seminar in Breslau. Wiesbaden, 1965. No. 289 a6.

96a] Luzzatto, Aldo: Hebraica Ambrosiana:I. Catalogue of Undescribed Hebrew Manuscripts in the Ambrosiana Library . . . (Milano), 1972, no. 39 (I).

97] Luzzatto, Samuel David: Bibliothèque de feu Joseph Almansi. In: Hebraeische Bibliographie, 4 (1861), p. 123.

98] Margoliouth, George: Catalogue of the Hebrew and Samaritan manuscripts in the British Museum. Part III. London, 1915, nos. 904 (IV).

99] Neubauer, Adolf; Arthur Ernest Cowley: Catalogue of the Hebrew manuscripts in the Bodleian library and in the college libraries of Oxford . . . Oxford, 1886–1906. Nos. 158 (5); 2496 (3); 2836 (6b)

ראה לעיל מס׳ 74, הערה.

100] Perreau, Pietro: Catalogo dei codici ebraici della Biblioteca di Parma non descritti dal de-Rossi. Firenze, 1880. Serie I, nos. 2 (9) F

210 r; 38 (2) F 11 r; 48 (4) F 126 v; Serie II, no. 50 (5).

101] Peyron, Bernardo: Codices Hebraici manu exarati Regaie bibliothecae quae in Taurinensi Athenaeo asservatur. Romae-Taurini-Florentiae, 1880. No. clxxvi. A. VI. 13 Fol. 54.
"Collection almost completely destroyed by fire in 1904" (cf. S. Shunami, Bibliography of Jewish bibliographies, 2nd ed., Jerusalem 1965, no. 3093).

102] Rossi, Giovanni, Bernardo de: Mss. codices hebraici biblioth. J.B. de Rossi . . . Accedit appendix qua continentur mss. codices reliqui al. linguarum. Parmae, 1803. Cod. 207 (1); 260; 327 (5); 770 (3); 772 (4); 1246 (9); Mss. Cod. Latini, Cod. 59 (12).
"Collection passed into possession of R. Biblioteca Palatina, Parma" (cf. S. Shunami, op. cit. no. 3078).

103] Roth, Ernst: Verzeichnis der orientalischen Handschriften in Deutschland; hebräische Handschriften, Teil 2. Wiesbaden, 1965. Harburg, no. 205 (III).

104] Sacerdote, Gustavo: Catalogo dei codici ebraici della Biblioteca casanatense. Firenze, 1897. No. 159 (II); 167 (I); 168 (III).

105] St[einschneider], M[oritz]: Hebraeische Handschriften in Parma. In: Hebraeische Bibliographie, 8 (1865), p. 96; 10 (1870), p. 100.

106] Id.: Catalog der hebräischen Handschriften in der Stadtbibliothek zu Hamburg und der sich anschliessenden in anderen Sprachen. Hamburg, 1878. No. 258 (2).

107] Id: [Die Handschriften-Verzeichnisse der K. Bibliothek zu Berlin. 2. Band:] Verzeichniss der hebräischen Handschriften. (Abt. [1]-2). Berlin, 1878-97. No. 24 (2).

108] Id.: Die hebraeischen Handschriften der K. Hof—und Staatsbibliothek in Muenchen. Nuenchen, 1875. No. 201 (7).
מהדורה ב מתוקנת ומורחבת: מינכן 1895.

111] Id.: . . . Flavius Mithridates . . . In: Hebraeische Bibliographie, vol. 21 (1881-82) p. 114.

112] Id: Christliche Hebräisten: Flavius Mithridates. In: Zeitschrift für Hebraeische Bibliographie, vol. 3 (1898), p. 154, no. 284.
על התרגום הלטיני של מאמר תחיית המתים מאת המומר פלאוויוס מיטרידאטס, מורהו בקבלה של פיקו דללה מיראנדולה. עיין עליו מחקריו של ח. וירשובסקי: פלאוויוס מיתרידאטס, בתוך: "דברי האקדמיה הלאומית הישראלית למדעים", כרך א, חוברת ג, ירושלים תשכ"ד; נוסח קדום של פירוש מורה נבוכים על דרך הקבלה לר' אברהם אבולעפיה בתרגומו הלאטיני של פלאוויוס מיתרידאטס, שם, כרך ג, חוברת ה, תשכ"ט.

113] Id.: Die hebr. Uebersetzungen des Mittelalters. Berlin, 1893. p. 431.

114] Id.: Die arabische Literatur der Juden. Frankfurt a.M., J. Kaufmann, 1902, p. 210.

Additions and corrections by S. Poznanski: "Zur juedisch-arabischen Literatur", in: Orientalische Literatur-Zeitung, 7 (1904), col. 351. Reprint: Berlin 1904.

114a] Wirszubski, Chaim: Flavius Mithridates Sermo de Passione Domini. Jerusalem: Israel Academy of Sciences and Humanities, 1963, p. 51.

115] Wolf, Johann Christoph: ר' משה בן מימון R. Mosche fil. Maimon h.e. Maimonides. In: Thesaurus Antiquitatum Sacrarum" (ed. Blaisio Ugolino), vol. 8. Venice, 1747. col. DCXCV.
Appeared originally in his *Bibliotheca Hebraea*, vols. 1 and 3. Hamburgi & Lipsiae, 1715-1727.

116] Zotenberg, Hermann: Catalogues des manuscrits hébreux et samaritains de la Bibliothèque impériale. Paris, 1866. No. 262 (3); 333 (2).

## INDEX (authors, editors and translators)

אבולעאפיה, מאיר 30־32
אברבנאל, יצחק 33
אברהם בן שלמה 34
אהרן בן משלם מלוניל 31, 35
אוריין, מ. 47
[אייגס, יהודה] 16, 21, 23, 27
אלוני, נ. 83
אלחריזי, יהודה 48, 55, 74, 229
אלשקר, ר' משה 35א
בחיי בן אשר 36
בנעט, ד. צ. 48־49
ברון, ש. 57
ברט, א. 50
בר־יוסף, מ. 25, 28
ברלינר, א. 44, 84, 89
ברמן, א. ז. 51
גוטמן, י. י. 52
גולדבלום, י. 86
דוד, א. 84א
דוראן, שמעון בן צמח 37
דינסטאג, י. י. 84 א־ב

דניאל הבבלי 75
האלפרין, ש. 14־15
הלברשטאם, ש. ז. ח. 53, 71
הלקין, א. ש. 78, 229
הרכבי, א. א. 11, 44, 72
וייס, א. ה. 54
זכריה בן ברכאל 75
זנה, י. 55, 57 78
זק"ש ש. 56, 85
טולידאנו, ב. 46
טייכר, י. ל. 57, 72, 78
טריוויש, י. א. 16, 19
יאפ"ז ראה: גולדבלום, י.
יוסף בן יואל 74
יעקבוביץ י. 78
ישראל בעל שם טוב 61
כהנא, ק. 58
לוינגר, ד. ש. 83, 96
לוצאטו, ש. ד. 59, 97
ליבוביץ, י. 50, 60
ליפשיץ, יעקב הלוי 60א

משה בן מימון 38־39
משה בן נחמן 40
נתנאל בירב פיומי 63
עגנון, ש. י. 61
עזריה מן האדומים 41
עמדן, י. 7
פינס, ש. 62
פינקל, י. 17, 18, 20, 69, 92
קאסטעל, ד. 41
קאפח, י. 29, 63
רבינוביץ, מ. ד. 20, 22, 24
שולמן, ק. 64
שלום, אברהם בן יצחק 42
שלום, ג. 44, 65
שמואל בן עלי 39, 72, 75
שמשון בן אברהם משאנץ 31, 43
ששת בן יצחק הנשיא 44
תבון, יהודה ן' 74
תבון, שמואל ן' 1־11, 13־28, 45,
49, 55, 57, 74
תנחום ירושלמי 46

Assemani, S.E. & J.S. 87
Bacher, W. 66
Baron, S.W. 66a
Bartolocci, G. 88
Berliner, A. 44, 89
Berman, L.V. 51
Bernheimer, C. 89a
Capua, A. di 90
Cowley, A.E. 99
Dassovius, T. 67
Dienstag, J.I. 67a-b
Dukes, L. 91
Eisenmenger, J.A. 68
Finkel, J. 17, 69, 92
Freimann, A. 93
Goldfeld, Lea Naomi 68a
Graetz, H. 44
Guttmann, J. 70

Halberstam, S.J. 71
Harkavy, A. 72
Hirschfeld, H. 94
Kohler, K. 73
Loewe, H. 95
Loewinger, D.S. 96
Luzzatto, A. 96a
Luzzatto, S.D. 97
Margoliouth, G. 98
Marx, A. 44
Mithridates, F. 111-112
Morais, S. 12
Neubauer, A. 71, 74, 99
Perreau, P. 100
Peyron, B. 101
Polinsky, M. 29א
Poznanski, S. 75, 114
Rosner, F. 29ג

Rossi, G.B. de 102
Roth, E. 103
Sacerdote, G. 104
Saracheck, J. 76
Silver, D.J. 77
Sonne, I. 78
Steinschneider, M. 78a,
105-114
Teicher, J.L. 72
Twersky, I. 78b
Waxman, M. 79
Weinryb, B.D. 96
Weiss, A. 80
Wiener, M. 69, 81
Wirszubski, C. 114a
Wolf, J.C. 115
Wolfson, H.A. 82
Zotenberg, H. 116

# Index of Scriptural and Talmudic Citations

*Genesis*
| | |
|---|---|
| 13:16 | 84 |
| 15:15 | 98 |
| 18:8 | 27 |
| 21:33 | 21, 52 |
| 26:3 | 84 |
| 28:13 | 84 |

*Exodus*
| | |
|---|---|
| 4:3 | 62 |
| 4:4 | 50, 69 |
| 4:6 | 44, 65 |
| 7:10 | 44, 65 |
| 7:12 | 46, 67 |
| 9:6 | 49, 69 |
| 9:16 | 46, 67 |
| 9:24 | 49, 69 |
| 9:26 | 49, 69 |
| 10:14 | 49, 69 |
| 13:17 | 47, 68 |
| 13:21 | 44, 65 |
| 14:27 | 50, 69 |
| 14:31 | 67 |
| 16:29 | 54 |
| 19 | 44, 65 |
| 19:9 | 67 |
| 19:21 | 64 |
| 34:28 | 55 |

*Leviticus*
| | |
|---|---|
| 17:14 | 58 |
| 26 | 49, 68, 69 |
| 26:21 | 49, 69 |
| 26:27–28 | 50, 69 |

*Numbers*
| | |
|---|---|
| 15:31 | 55, 66 |

| | |
|---|---|
| 16:30 | 62 |
| 16:33 | 50, 69 |
| 18:28 | 100 |
| 20:10 | 19 |

*Deuteronomy*
| | |
|---|---|
| 1:8 | 84 |
| 1:28 | 62 |
| 4:19–20 | 48, 69 |
| 5:21 | 46, 67 |
| 6:4 | 22, 60 |
| 6:24 | 68 |
| 11:9 | 84 |
| 11:21 | 84 |
| 17:11 | 54 |
| 22:7 | 55, 66 |
| 28 | 49, 68, 69 |
| 28:46 | 48, 68 |
| 29:3 | 47, 68 |
| 32:27 | 84 |
| 32:39 | 97 |
| 33:26 | 66 |

*I Samuel*
| | |
|---|---|
| 2:6 | 84 |
| 12:17–18 | 49, 69 |
| 16:7 | 53 |

*II Samuel*
| | |
|---|---|
| 2:6 | 57 |
| 14:14 | 42 |

*I Kings*
| | |
|---|---|
| 13:3 | 49, 69 |
| 13:4 | 62 |
| 13:5 | 49, 69 |
| 19:8 | 55 |

*Isaiah*
4:13            100
11:6            37, 60, 61
11:9            37, 39, 61, 62
11:19           37, 61
26:11           84
26:19           60, 64, 98
28:9            26, 56
28:13           51, 70
29:11           37, 61
38:17           54
38:18—19        42
42:11           84

*Jeremiah*
13:23           43, 65

*Ezekiel*
17:2            61
27:10           84
37              33, 58

*Hosea*
6:2             84
12:11           61

*Psalms*
50:4—5          84
68:4            66
72:16           84, 90
78:39           42, 64
88:11           42, 43—44, 64
104:30          84
115:5—6         34, 60

*Proverbs*
1:6             62
8:8             21, 52
8:9             21, 52
9:9             51, 70
12:23           21, 52

*Job*
1:21            42, 64

7:9             42, 78, 84
13:5            34, 60
14:13—15        98
14:14           19, 41, 43

*Lamentations*
1:12            26, 55

*Ecclesiastes*
1:9             91
3:14            39, 63
3:19 ff.        78, 98
9:4—6           84
12:7            43, 64

*Daniel*
12              60, 61, 63
12:1—4          98
12:2            32, 43, 44, 45, 57, 65,
                66, 84
12:13           32, 42, 44, 45, 65, 66, 84

*Ben Sira*
41:3 ff.        78, 99

*Berachoth*
5a              48, 69
17a             25, 34, 55, 84, 86, 90, 98
18b             57
31b             56
34b             38, 61
60a             39, 63

*Shabbath*
63a             38, 61
77b             55
97a             60
151b            38, 61
156a            48, 68
156b            48, 68

*Pesachim*
119b            28

*Yoma*
19b            60

*Chagigah*
7a             53
12a            66
13a            28
22b            88

*Ketuboth*
29a            83, 98

*Nedarim*
37a            53

*Kiddushin*
39b            26, 66
62a            88

*Baba Metzia*
59b            39, 63

*Baba Bathra*
16a            57, 78, 98

*Sanhedrin*
64b            55, 66
90a            57, 87
90b            22, 42, 55, 65
90b–91a        84
90b–92a        84
91b            42, 65, 98

*92a*           42, 65
92b            33, 59, 87, 100
99a            84
106b           22
108a           87

*Abodah Zarah*
4:7            55
2b             67
26a            84
54b            39, 62

*Aboth*
4:5            62, 84
5:5            39, 62
5:6            65

*Chullin*
90b            39, 62, 87

*Genesis Rabbah*
5:4            65
13             58

*Exodus Rabbah*
21:6           65

*Sifra*
Metzorah       51, 70

*Song of Songs Rabbah*
1:1:8          62

# Index of References to Works by Maimonides

*Guide for the Perplexed,* 10, 11, 23, 27,
   28, 35, 38, 44, 45, 46, 52, 72, 74, 76,
   77, 82
1:26           35, 56, 60
1:33–35        28, 57
1:41           35, 60, 63

1:46           55, 59
1:49           27, 56
1:58           70
1:70           66
1:71           57
1:72           59

1:78          70
2:6           27, 56
2:10          27, 56
2:14          55
2:17          45
2:22          61
2:23          45, 61, 65
2:25          44, 45, 65, 67
2:28          70
2:29          62, 63, 65
2:33          28, 57
2:47          28, 57
3:11          62
3:29          66
3:31          18
3:32          67, 68
3:36          69
3:37          18
3:45          46, 66
3:50          28, 57

*Mishneh Torah,* 14, 15, 17, 24, 32, 36,
45, 52, 63, 72, 74, 76, 79, 80, 83, 88,
96, 101

*Hilchoth Yesodei HaTorah*
1:1           54
1:7           45, 65
1:7–9         54
1:11–12       56
2:8–10        70
4:3           64
4:3–4         59
4:9           63

*Hilchoth Abodah Zarah*
2:4           99
2:7           80, 98, 99
4:2           80
4:2–4         98

*Hilchoth Teshubah*
3:6–14        55

3:7           56
3:10–14       41, 64
8             54, 55, 58
8:1           25, 55
8:2           55, 57, 82, 98
8:3           55
9             55, 58

*Hilchoth Tefillin*
1:11          98

*Hilchoth Berachot*
1:1           98

*Hilchoth Shabbath*
2:1           98
20:7          98

*Hilchoth Kiddush Ha-Chodesh*
4:16          98, 99

*Hilchoth Shemita Ve-Yovel*
13:13         18

*Hilchoth Milah*
3:6           98

*Hilchoth Parah Adumah*
11:2          88

*Hilchoth Issurei Bi'ah*
14:3–5        18
15:2          98
15:3          83

*Hilchoth Melachim*
2:1           61
11:3          36, 61
12:1          61, 62

*Commentary on the Mishnah,* 1, 23, 32,
33, 37, 41, 51, 52, 54, 55, 63

*Chagigah* 2:1, 56

*Sanhedrin*, 1, 15, 54, 77, 79
*Perek Chelek*, 1, 15, 19, 24, 52, 55, 56, 58, 63
Eight Chapters, 59, 65, 70

*Treatise on Resurrection*, 1, 3, 82, 87
Arabic text, 7, 8, 9, 10, 13, 14
Hebrew text, 7, 8, 9, 10, 12, 13

English translations, 8, 14
Manuscripts, 7, 8, 9, 12, 13
Finkel's edition, 7, 8, 9, 10
Rabbinowitz's edition, 10, 11
Kafih's edition, 12, 13
forgery theory, 11–12, 13
contents and purpose, 15–20
annotated translation, 21–51

# Index of Names

Aaron ben Meshullam, 81–82, 83, 85, 87, 90
Ablet, 68
Abraham bar Ḥiyya, 19
Abraham ben Nathan of Lunel (Abraham ben Nathan ha-Yarhi), 87, 89, 90
Abraham ben Solomon, 7
Abraham of Toul, 85
Abu al Birkat Hibat Allah, 58
Albo, Joseph, 78
Alfakhar, Judah, 77
*Al Farabi* (Steinschneider), 58
al-Ḥarizi, Judah. *See* Ḥarizi, Judah al-,
*Alef Bet de R. Akiba*, 95
*Arabischer Litteratur* (Steinschneider), 58
Aristotle, 39, 62, 65, 93
Ashi, Rav, 81

Baneth, D. Z., 10, 11, 12, 53, 57
Bahya ibn Pakuda, 77

Caleb, Rabbi, 89

*Derech Hashem* (Luzzatto), 4
David of Chateaux Thierry, 85
Dienstag, Jacob, 1, 14

Eliezer ben Aaron of Bourgogne, 85
Eliezer ben R. Yose the Galilean, 59
Emden, Yaakov, 5
*Emunot ve De'ot* (Saadya), 82, 87
Epicurus, 93

Finkel, Joshua, 7, 8, 9, 10, 11, 12, 13, 14, 15, 19, 53, 55, 58, 59, 60, 61

Graetz, H., 100

Halevi, Samuel, 30, 31, 58
Ḥarizi, Judah al-, 7, 8, 9, 10, 11, 12, 13, 82
*Hebraeisch, Bibliographie* (Steinschneider), 7
Hibbat Allah ibn Malkan, 58
Hippocrates, 59

Ibn Aknin, 52
Ibn Balam, 37, 61
Ibn Ezra, 19, 61
Ibn Ganach, Jonah, 61
Ibn Gekatila, Moses, 37
Ibn Sina, 31
Ibn Tibbon, Judah, 82
Ibn Tibbon, Samuel, 7, 8, 9, 11, 12, 13, 21, 59

Isaac ben Abraham of Dampierre, 85
Isaac ben Samuel, 90

Jonathan ha-Kohen, 79–80, 81, 83
Joseph ben Joel, 7, 8, 9, 10, 11, 12
Judah, Rabbi, 58

Kafih, Joseph, 12–13, 14, 20
*Kitab al Rasail* (Meir b. Todros), 72, 89, 91, 95

"Literary Forgery in the Thirteenth Century" (Teicher), 11
Luzzatto, Moshe Chayim, 4, 5

*Maimonidean Criticism and the Maimonidean Controversy* (Silver), 1, 20, 71
Maimonides, Abraham, 88–89
Maimonides, Moses, 1, 4, 9, 15–20, 71, 77, 79, 90
  Works. *See* Index of References to Works by Maimonides
*Malbim* (Meir Leib ben Yechiel Micha'el), 3–4
Meir ben Sheshet ha-Nasi, 7, 9, 10
Meir ben Todros Abulafia, 71, 72–76, 79–80, 81, 82, 83, 84, 85, 86, 88, 89, 90, 91, 92
*Milhamot Adonai* (Abraham Maimonides), 89
Morais, S., 8
Moses ha-Kohen, 80, 83
Munk, Solomon, 7
*Murshid* (Tanḥum Yerushalmi), 7

Nachmanides, 5, 71

*On Animals* (Aristotle), 39, 62

Palquera, Shem Tob, 54
Philo, 98

Plato, 93
Polinsky, Milton, S., 14

Raba, 78
Rabad, 80, 83
Rabbinowitz, Mordecai Dov, 10, 11, 12, 14, 19–20, 52, 53, 54, 56, 57, 58, 59, 60, 61, 62, 63, 64, 65, 66, 67, 68, 69, 70
Rabbina, 81
Radak, 61
Regenworm, Miriam, 2

Saadya, 77, 87, 90
Samuel (talmudic sage), 68
Samuel ben Ali, 16
Sarachek, J., 89
*Sefer Kenaot* (Meir b. Todros), 72
Sheshet ben Isaac Benveniste (Sheshet ha-Nasi ben Isaac of Saragossa), 91–94, 95, 96, 97
*Shiur Komah,* 95
Silver, Jeremy, 1, 19, 20, 71
Simson ben Abraham of Sens, 85, 86–89, 90
Simson of Corbeil, 85
Solomon ben Abraham of Montpellier, 71
Solomon of Meroz, 85
Steinschneider, Moritz, 7, 58

*Takhemoni* (Harizi), 8, 9
Tanḥum Yerushalmi, 7
Teicher, Y. L., 11, 12
*Treatise on Future Reward* (Ibn Sina), 30–31
Twerski, Aaron, 1

Zacuto, Abraham, 89
Zerahyah ha-Yevani, 77
Zona, Y., 10, 11, 12

## About the Author

**FRED ROSNER, M.D., F.A.C.P.,** is Director of the Department of Medicine of the Mount Sinai Services at the Queens Hospital Center and Professor of Medicine at New York's Mount Sinai School of Medicine. He is a diplomate of the American Board of Internal Medicine and a Fellow of the American College of Physicians. He is the recipient of numerous awards.

Dr. Rosner is an internationally known authority on medical ethics. He has lectured widely on Jewish medical ethics and is in great demand as a speaker on this and related topics. He has served as a visiting professor and lecturer in England, France, Germany, Mexico, Canada, Holland, Israel, South Africa, and throughout the United States. He is a member of the Professional Advisory Board of the prestigious Kennedy Institute for Ethics, Georgetown University. He is also Chairman of the Medical Ethics Committee of the Medical Society of the State of New York.

He is the author of five widely acclaimed books on Jewish medical ethics including *Modern Medicine and Jewish Ethics* (2nd enlarged edition, Ktav 1991), *Medicine and Jewish Law Volume I* (Aronson 1990), and *Medicine and Jewish Law Volume II* (Aronson 1993). These books are up-to-date examinations of the Jewish view on many important bioethical issues in medical practice. Dr. Rosner is also a noted Maimonidean scholar and has translated and published in English most of Maimonides' medical writings.